sweet Social Media

VALERIO CIRELLA

Ordering Information:

Special discounts are available on quantity purchases by corporations, associations, and others. For details, contact the publisher at the address above.

First Published, July 2015

This revised edition published February 2016

For Luca and Julian

Index

Acknowledgements

Some people fight every day for their freedom and for people freedom. Most of them are silent heroes among us and they not ask for award or popularity; they fight for believes and right. I want thank those people, which serve the interests of society trying to make a world a better place to live.

List of Figures

List of Tables

Abbreviation

AI =   Artificial Intelligence

FB =   Face Book

SM =   Social Media

SMM =   Social Media Marketing

SN / SNs =   Social Network / Social Networks

TM =   Traditional Media

SROI =   Social Return Of Investment

Introduction

By

Valerio Cirella & Mario Cirella[1]

This book offers the essential information about social media, it does not contain highly technical information or analytical formulas but, in contrast, it offers an explanation of the new communication system and also provides ideas to spark off individual researches.

I wanted to create a book that was simple, effective and brief; focused on analyses and explanations of social media's meaning, the idea behind them, and the influence they have on people's lives.

Social media (SM) system is a next step of the Internet evolution and it represents the result of the interaction between new *communication needs and technology development* (based on the Internet).

Many important events occurred in the USA in 1969. For example, the military operations in Vietnam, the moon landing, the election of Nixon as the 37th President of the United States, and the Woodstock concert. However, few remember that in that year four American universities connected their PCs

---

[1] Mario Cirella is a retired sociologist, journalist and telecommunication specialist.

together in one single network. This network was the civil implementation of an original military project, designed by ARPA (Advanced Research Project Agency). This military project had the purpose to keep the Pentagon information up and running also after a hypothetical nuclear attack from foreign countries. This because the multiple locations, connected each other, provided a solution of disaster recovery where essential data were stored in different places and restored if needed.

The Internet came years later when it became easier to connect networks using the TCP/IP protocol, and it became popular with the development of browsers and search engines.

Initially, the Internet was conceived and developed to connect only machines, and to allow the exchange of information to make jobs easier and economically convenient for companies. In just a few years, this technology affected company business on the one hand, and people's socialisation, interests and mobility on the other.

Some people made a lot of money from the Internet, and new companies, were created, for example: Larry Page and Sergey Brin (Google founders); Jeff Bezos (Amazon founder); Masayoshi Son (President of SoftBank); Pierre Omidyar (eBay founder and chairman); Hiroshi Mikitani (Rakuten co-founder and CEO); Mark Zuckerberg (co-founder of Facebook); Ma Huateng (founder of Tencent Inc.).

The Internet is only a technology, and therefore impersonal, but social media (SM) have changed this trait. SM category is made up of many 'mediums' (for this reason I will always address SM as a plural), which will be discussed individually in this book. They have enriched the 'Information Age' and they are pushing the society toward one based on 'digital interactions between people'.

SM were created to support the circulation of information between people, who need to register their profile and prove their identity for the interactions. For example, it is possible to login to some websites, or sell products and services, using a personal Internet profile from another website (e.g. using the personal Facebook or LinkedIn profile). In order to keep and develop business and social relationships with hundreds of contacts, SM usage is growing because they are:

a) Handy;
b) Cheap;
c) Effective.

One different opinion is Solis, who stated in 2007: *"Social Media is about Sociology and not Technology"*. He sustains that any media, in general, exists because they are used for people's interactions and, furthermore, a medium is developed to reach people and not an audience.

This book analyses this kind of statements and ideas, verifying the importance of technology and if it plays an important role in increasing the usage of SM. Nowadays, it looks like the development of technology supports the increase of the human interactions, for example: mobile phones and software applications, tablet computers, fast Internet connections, and the ability to send content as a combination of images and audio.

During my research, I found a very interesting quote: *"We don't have a choice on whether we do social media, the question is how well we do it."* (Qualman, 2010). In summary, the author's message is that SM represent *"the biggest shift since the Industrial Revolution"*. I completely support this definition because, as I demonstrate in this book, the implementation of SM has changed major aspects of our society and economy. They are so powerful that they can hurt or promote people and companies' reputations, and change the quality of services or their perception.

Other authors, like Centorrino and Romero (2012) believe that SM have redefined communication in terms of time and space (distance), because they have created new places for meetings and a new way to interact, watch TV, listen to music, read a newspaper, or get an education or training.

Specifically, they are part of a group of theorists who believe that the Internet has compressed time and space (in terms of distance) between users, just as all previous systems of transportation have done. For example, when the railways were developed, they reduced the time and space needed to transport goods and people and, years later, the development of airplane reduced the two elements even more. This means that the progress and developments of technology contribute to reduce the importance and the role of Time and Space in the transportation system. Same analogy can be used for the communication. Indeed, in the past the creation and development of new methods of communication (e.g. papyrus, smoke signals and letters) had both purpose of reducing the time needed by message to travel and to spread the message over the distance. The Internet has given a big contribution in this sense, because it makes possible to distribute the message quickly and over a long distance.

In this case, the Internet represents the vehicle, which transport the message (e.g. information, songs, pictures, documents, opinions and e-books, commands and instructions), and SM are a methods of communication.

For one of the world's most prominent social theorists, Bauman (2000), time and space compression also affects the transformation of people's lives. He explains that people use SM for different reasons, for example for buying, interacting with others, finding and providing information, and for playing; this use affects people's behaviour and habits. One of the most interesting of Bauman's views is that the modern society is becoming 'exterritorial and not more contained by the space'. Specifically, the element of 'space' is about to disappear from our society because it is becoming less important than it was a few years ago.

To explain this point more effectively, let's analyse four different ways to communicate between people: a face–to-face conversation implies that two or more people are in close proximity (space has a primary role in this case). If they decide to communicate with a letter, the social interaction is compressed into words on paper, the letter takes time to reach the receiver and it has a space (distance) to cover before reaching the destination. In contrast, an email drastically reduces the time needed for the interaction and the space is non influential for the purpose of communication. If the same people decide to communicate using online chat, well, the two elements (time and space) are almost non-existent.

The continuous technology evolution makes people's habits dynamic, and this changes our society's organisation creating a 'Liquid Society'. Bauman also suggests that SM have created a double life, because in addition the real one, there is a digital one. For example, people can socialise with friends in one place and be also connected to another network, using tweets, instant chats, business emails, dating applications, picture postings and tags.

A scary or intriguing part (depending on the personal view of the 'the Internet evolution') is that personal opinions, tastes, interests, and hobbies are exposed and available to almost everyone with the Internet access, and this makes it easier to recreate and analyse identities.

SM can show also other information such as: places visited and time of visit, current employer name, date of birth, current living city, siblings and many others. This also means that personal life can be available for comments, to be recalled at any time in a discussion or comment and also saved...just in case.

Chapter One

Social Media Today

This chapter opens with a definition of social media and with a list of medium which are part of this category. The main arguments are around what the most popular medium is nowadays, and how and why it has become successful.

The main success of social media is due to social networks, which are based on the theory of *"six degrees of separation"*. Social media are also used in many situations and for different scopes that will be described in the last section.

1.1 Phenomenon Definition

In my view, **social media** *are virtual communities and networks that support the communication and the sharing of ideas and data between people (users).*

Social media (SM) represent the newest media developed and used nowadays for communication between people. The most common social platforms used are quite young: for example, MySpace was founded in 2003, Facebook in 2004, YouTube in 2005, and Twitter in 2006. The full potential and comprehension of this new way of communication is not yet well perceived by the majority of people.

While they are used widely — for example, Facebook has an average of 802 m daily active users (Facebook, 2014), LinkedIn has 300 m members (LinkedIn, 2014), and WhatsApp has more than 100 m users (Forbes, 2012) — only a reduced number of users know what SM really represent today from a political, economic and social point of view. Instead, the majority of users associate SM only with social networks (SNs) or online news channels.

This chapter explains what the differences are between SM and SNs. As a starting point, Sterne (2010) defines SM as a group of Medium, which is represented in Fig. 1.

Source: Team YS, 2013

Figure 1 – SM channels

The following details give greater clarifications on each role and characteristic:

- **Social Blogs and Weblogs**. These are websites run by an individual or small group of writers, which provide comments or news on facts and events that would interest a particular community. Usually, blogs create information and support idea–sharing, and readers can post comments regarding the topics covered.
- **Microblogging**. These are blogs that use a limited number of characters. The most well-known one is Twitter, which uses only 140 characters per message.
- **Social Bookmarking**. These are websites that are focused on bookmarks and web documents that users can share and edit. Pinterest, Digg and Fark are examples of social bookmarking. There is not shared data, but only references to other web pages. Typically, public libraries use those platforms to speed up catalogue research.
- **Internet Forums**. These are websites, or parts of websites, dedicated to specific topics such as getting advice or solving problems. For example, mobile phone providers have webpages dedicated to providing information such as: service numbers and the procedure to deactivate/activate a service. Other examples are: Yahoo Forums, and boards on the WikiHow.com website.
- **Rating.** The most common are the ones used to book holidays, review restaurants and buy goods (e.g. eBay, Amazon, Airbnb and Alibaba).

In addition to the list above, there are other categories to consider, such as:

- **Social Networks (SNs)**. These are applications dedicated to people's connections (personal and/or professional). Users invite people to join their network in order to read their professional and private life updates and progression, and to seek opinions and information. SNs support interactions between users through the sharing of: comments, opinions, videos, images and personal status updates. SNs are convenient because they are cheap or free, and quick and easy to use. They are either public or private (invitation only) communities. In this category, instant chat applications are also included because they share the same characteristics: they allow connections and sharing of digital material.

- **Sharing Platforms**. Examples are: OneDrive, Dropbox, Google Drive and YouTube. These are cloud applications, which allow the uploading and downloading of digital content and to view streaming content.

Marketing Charts (2015) reports the ranking of most used social media website of September 2015 and, from this particular list, Facebook is the leader, followed by You Tube and Twitter (see Fig. 2).

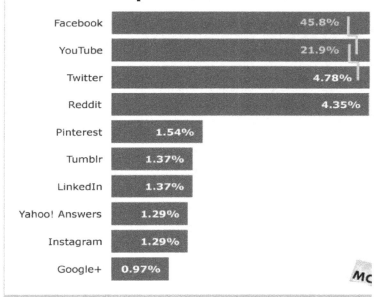

Top 10 Multi-Platform Social Networking Websites & Forums
by US Market Share of Visits (%)
browser-based (excluding in-app) visits across PC and mobile combined
September 2015

Facebook	45.8%
YouTube	21.9%
Twitter	4.78%
Reddit	4.35%
Pinterest	1.54%
Tumblr	1.37%
LinkedIn	1.37%
Yahoo! Answers	1.29%
Instagram	1.29%
Google+	0.97%

MarketingCharts.com | Data Source: Experian Marketing Services

Source: Marketing Charts, 2015

Figure 2 - Top 10 Visited Multi-Platform Social-Networking Websites & Forum

1.1.1 Facebook

Facebook (FB) is the market leader of SNs, with a really impressive popularity. According to the company's data release, FB had 1.01 billion daily active users on average for September 2015. It is an American company but the 83.5% of the daily users are based outside USA & Canada.

FB was founded by Mark Zuckerberg, a Harvard student, with the initial idea to profile students and staff of his college. Soon, the website became very popular and he extended access to other colleges, and gradually the application became international and accessible to everyone.

The original business idea, which made Facebook a $ 2.5 b company (Facebook, 2014), was created and developed without market research or a business plan.

There are few points that make Facebook the number one in the entire SM:

1. The founder believes strongly in the realisation of an idea; the best business idea is nothing without an execution.
2. The FB application is easy to use and intuitive. When the company decides to improve the web site, the simplicity is the first approach.
3. Service is reliable (minor crashes) and easy to access. Since its creation, FB has moved forward, but always keeps in mind to guarantee access to the service.
4. Focus on the product and service quality. Zuckerberg always been focused on his product, considering profits as less important. In this way, the company creates a real value for customers, and this leads to the generation of more business by itself.
5. Hire and retain the best employees on the market and be ready to replace them when needed. This has contributed to developing FB to be the successful company it is today.
6. Zuckerberg has had full company control since the company was created. This has helped the company growth because decisions are made quickly and the company vision is clear and achievable.

7. Keep the focus on innovation in order to keep the business going. FB is a company which invests in new applications or services (e.g. news feed, Facebook Messenger, video calls) and acquiring new companies (WhatsApp).
8. FB has long-term goals and it is not focused exclusively on profit. Since the beginning of company's creation, the founder believed in the company's future and its potential business growth. This made him continue working and achieving big successes.

1.1.2 YouTube

Founded in 2005, YouTube is the most popular platform for video sharing. It was created by three young entrepreneurs: Chad Hurley, Steve Chen, and Jawed Karim. In 2006, the company grew quickly, thanks to the increase of users and a business partnership with NBC for marketing and advertising. Late in 2006 the company was acquired by Google for $1.65 b in stock.

Key success factors:

1. It is perceived as the first online on-demand TV. Users are free to search any topic they want.
2. It is easy to use, available and easy to access.
3. Zero or low streaming latency. No need to download the application, and there are no pop-ups.
4. Its popularity also increases the number and the quality of videos available on the platform.

1.1.3 Twitter

Twitter is a SN that provides a microblogging service. A registered user can "tweet" a maximum of 140 characters. The company was founded in 2006 and soon gained popularity, with 320 m of active users for September 2015 (Twitter, 2016). According to eMarketer (2014), active US Twitter accounts will grow even more in the coming years. In particular, the expectations are:

1. The growing number of users over the years (from 36.2 m in 2012 to 64.9 m in 2018).
2. The positive trend year on year for:
   a) Compared to the overall SNs population, Twitter expectation is to grow from 23% of 2008 to 34% in 2018.

   b) Compared to the Internet users' population, Twitter users will grow from 15.2% of 2012 to 24.2% of 2018.

The data above relates to the US market and to the period from 2012 to 2018. The analysis assumes that users log into their account from any device at least once per month.

Twitter is an application for different ages but18 to 24 year olds use it the most (eMarketer, 2014).

The reasons for this and what makes Twitter a popular application are:

1. With Twitter it is possible to send short messages to "followers", with a maximum 140 characters (140 for the message and 20 for username), and this makes the application appealing for some users, because this limitation protects the followers from receiving annoying multiple texts per tweet.

2. Twitter simplifies staying in touch with friends or finding new ones with common interests (e.g. sports, politics and events).
3. It is effective for businesses because they can communicate more easily with customers, who provide opinions on services and products purchased.
4. People use the application as a source of information about upcoming products or to improve their skills because it is possible to find or stay in touch with experts.

1.2 Why now?

During my research and analysis the most common two questions I heard from acquaintances were: "Why are SM so popular today?" and "What is the reason for such interest?"

The answers are related to the importance of SNs to SM.

History tells that the first SN (on the internet) was **Sixdegrees.com**, which was developed in 1997 and named after the *"six degrees of separation"* theory. This theory states that any person in the world is connected with everyone else within just six connections.

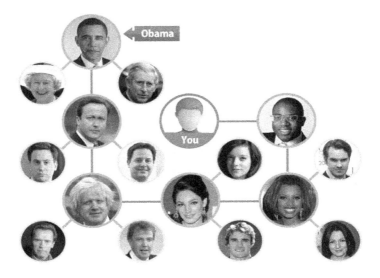

Source: Ericrettberg.com, 2014

Figure 3 - "Six Degrees of Separation" Concept

Based on this concept, Sixdegrees.com had features that facilitated users to invite family, friends and external contacts, and to show the link between people that joined the network.

At that time, Sixdegrees.com was not a big success, in contrast with the popularity of the idea today.

This is because at that time, the Internet was not very popular. Indeed, people failed to recognise the benefits of the Internet applications, and saw instead a threat to privacy.

SNs, and SM, in general, become popular when the social and economic conditions changed and, in particular, when:

1. More online applications were created.

2. Entrepreneurs recognised the importance, and the economic opportunity, to establish new connections.
3. Dating websites and online newspapers became popular.
4. The Internet connection fees went down, increasing the Internet penetration.
5. Globalisation boomed and people needed to stay in contact with their loved ones.
6. Applications were created for mobile phones to stay in contact with friends.
7. People were able to watch streaming programs anytime and anywhere.
8. Companies became interested in this new growing business and invested in publicity and software applications, creating new jobs and increasing the quality of products.

In brief, SM popularity and interest were developed by three key elements: entertainment need, technology progress and overall benefit for users.

Those three elements are related and they have been developing together until consumers (users) found SM exciting, stimulating, and beneficial. Specifically:

1. Need to satisfy **Entertainment.** SM offer an opportunity for people to kill time, to relax, to emote, to feel happy, to learn, to fill short or long period of solitude. This can be get through SNs, video, e-book or music App.
2. **Technology progress.** This supports the positive trends of SM with simple and interesting software applications and affordable devices. Technology also creates stimuli to develop and use SM because research

could make new devices available that could support better software applications. Moreover, technology costs decrease; mobile devices, such as mobile phones, tablets and laptops, increase their variety and quality and improving their aesthetics.

3. **Benefit.** The SM industry has been capable to develop the platform that most interest the public. For example, the first SN developed the idea of having a community of friends in one logical location that is easy to reach and to stay connected with. Furthermore, any interaction can be established at any place, any time and for a reasonable price. Companies are investing in SM because they are an extraordinary source of consumer data and are also self-updated. Companies and people can be "followed" by other users, thereby quantifying their importance in the global community. For example, a movie producer would take into consideration the number of followers an actor has in order to estimate a film's viewing figures and sales, or a politician could anticipate a vote's trend or test the consensus of a political idea.

    In addition, market researchers look favourably on these media because consumers can be targeted better. Companies can reach potential customers more easily and with specific messages and offers, thus avoiding random emails. Users, which decide to "like" products generate awareness in their friends and become a free and valuable sponsor for other potential customers. Companies track consumers' activities and physical location to promote shops or goods close to their position.

1.3 Current Uses

SM are available and usable anytime and anywhere; it is a constant presence in people's lives without them even realising. In addition to that, mobile devices have boosted its popularity because there are now specific applications for any specific need. For example, there are applications to find and book a taxi (e.g. Hailo, GrabTaxi or Uber), to operate a personal bank account or to read a digital newspaper.

The major SM applications are created for:

1. **Entertainment.** SM offers a wide selection of entertainment applications. People use them to socialise (e.g. SNs and photo sharing), to be amused by a streaming event, to watch video content and to play games.
   For the games industry in particular SM is very lucrative; indeed, SNs have integrated games into their applications, and big companies like Sony and Microsoft are gaining profit by the integration of SM into their consoles and creating, with this, a new generation of gamers and gaming.

2. **Business.** SM provides the opportunity to reduce costs, improve risk management and enhance profits. This is possible because they support a global business: selling in rich and growing markets and producing in more convenient ones. Indeed, they are able to hire employees and establish headquarters in low wage and low cost countries around the world, and then connect employees with each other, creating a virtual workplace. From a SM perspective, this is possible because workers use, for example, videoconferencing, email, online chat and cloud applications.

There is another benefit to consider with the creation of a global connection: companies protect their business from possible failures or outages, due to, for example, fire, national strikes or public holidays.

Moreover, this global presence also creates a 24 h flow of income. In fact, as one side of the world sleeps, the other side is being productive.

Besides that, there is also the aspect of e-commerce, which is basically a 24 h shop. The warehouse is located in the most convenient city or country and delivers almost anywhere in the world.

As I mentioned above, SM can be used also to generate new business opportunities or, in the worst case, to protect from the risk of losing it. In fact, customers have more options if they decide to buy and companies are also closer to new generations of buyers, who use SM more and more for their purchases.

There are also companies that have a core business hinged on SM, such as developing new software applications and platforms for SM. Indeed, from 2003 to 2010 in the USA, the number of patents for SN reached 1,200, up from almost 0 in 2003 (Nowotarski, 2011).

SM offers benefits to consumers as well because they can contribute to reducing costs and optimising time. For example, through online chats, online purchases and emails, it is possible to avoid using the car, consuming fuel, paying for the car park, experiencing traffic jams and stress.

3. **Knowledge**. SM give the opportunity to spread information quickly across users. It is also used by traditional media, which they are trying to renovate and modernize their way to communicate the news to the public, in line with today technology and meet readers' needs. For example, in 1970 if we were far from our home country, it was almost impossible to read our favourite newspaper, follow our favourite football team, or watch our favourite program but it is something possible today thanks to the technology. Moreover, SM is one of the most valuable sources of information, where, for example, it is convenient to watch videos on how fix things in the house or car, to get new recipes and surprise family and friends, or get information on the sciences and the arts. All this is possible without ringing some specialist.

Chapter Two

The Rise of Social Media's Influence

This chapter analyses SM's influence on users' decisions and their differences from traditional media such as TV, radio and print. There is also a brief summary of the communication models and an analysis of the different typologies of media highlighted by Professor Innis. In specific, it will explain the difference between the media that promote decentralization and local culture and those that support communication over a distance and promote the spread of message, trade and centralization. These two types of media have been used by different imperialisms in the past in becoming architects of their fortunes.

2.1 Communication Essentials

People communicate to fulfil their needs and, according to Adler & Proctor II (2012), those are:

1. **Physical needs**. A positive communication is beneficial for wellbeing because it keeps all the

intellectual and memory functionalities active, improves the mood, reduces stress and gives the right motivation for the day.

2. **Identity needs**. Communication is also essential for self-evaluation and for improving personal skills, because it identifies personal weakness. Indeed, through a fair and honest confrontation with others, we can collocate ourselves in the community.

3. **Social needs**. Communication is also necessary for keeping and developing a social life, which increases life satisfaction and happiness. Interacting with other people increases personal motivation and builds relationships.

4. **Practical goals**. Communication is fundamental to fulfilling daily activities (e.g. performing a job, negotiating prices, or teaching kids how to ride a bicycle or to drink from a cup).

Aristotle identified one of the first simple and effective models of communication (Aristotle's model of communication), which is based on the following elements and connections:

Speaker → Speech → Occasion → Audience → Effect

This model was intended for public speaking, where the key role was occupied by the speaker. It is a one-way communication model and it is based on a message going out to influence an **audience** (receiver).

Since Aristotle, other communication models were created and elaborated on, and one in particular is widely accepted by social science, is known as the "Shannon–Weaver model of communication", and is shown in Fig. 4. It was created for data communication and adapted for social communication because it is very effective and adapts very well to other communication processes.

Shannon was an American mathematician, electronic engineer, and cryptographer, and Weaver was an American scientist, mathematician and science administrator. They developed this model to study the communication between two sources (sender and receiver) and spoke for the first time about *information source, message, transmitter, signal, channel, noise, receiver, information destination, probability of error, encoding, decoding, information rate, and channel capacity.*

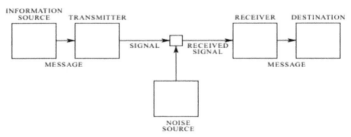

Source: Shannon, 1948

Figure 4 – Shannon-Weaver Model of Communication

Using the model above as a basis, more complex ones developed in order to depict communication in a specific context or to explain two-way communications using more elements. The main models are described below:

1) Linear Model of Communication

Social science adopted the essence of Shannon and Weaver's model to use it, for example, in education, organizational analysis and psychology.

The model in Fig. 5 was adapted to these fields, replacing the central part with the "channel" used by the communication (i.e. the medium through which the message passes).

In summary, the linear model moves from one person to another without feedback and includes the following elements:

a) **Information source**, which creates the message;
b) **Transmitter**, which converts the message into signals;
c) **Channel**, which is the medium used by message to reach the target;
d) **Receiver**, which "decodes" (reconstructs) the message from the signal;
e) **Destination**, where the message arrives;
f) **Noise**, which is the external sound that comes between the two subjects involved in the process.

It is possible to define this model with a few **main adjectives**, such as:

a) Simple, because the model has a few basic elements;
b) Quantifiable, because the transmission data can be quantified;
c) Effective for a one to one interaction, rather for a mass audience;
d) Not suitable for two-way communication;

e)   The concept is based on a primary role (sender) and a secondary (or passive) role (receiver).

2) Interactive Model

This models two-way communication and it is based on the linear model process. This means that the message goes from a sender to a receiver and the receiver became a sender for the reverse process.

Compared to the linear model, this supports proper communication because of the return of the communication (also called **feedback**). Indeed, this model supports the idea of exchanging data or information between two participants but, in contrast, the sender has to wait for the message to arrive at the receiver before he/she can receive a message back.

3) Transactional Model

This model is based on the interactive model, but also includes an environment concept. This means, two subjects engaged in communication can belong to different: *physical, cultural and personal* environments (e.g. different ethnic groups, job roles, ages, physical places or income) that can influence their communication.

The transactional model highlights that the **communication becomes more difficult as the differences between the speakers increase**.

The "channel" has also a special importance for the communication because the same message can cause different feelings in the receiver based on the media used for the transmission. For example, if I say: "*I love you*" to my wife, I know that I will influence her feelings, but this feeling is different if I communicate the same message by email or with a romantic card.

In Fig. 5 there is a representation of this model, which proposes the same elements of interactive model, but with two differences:

1. The inclusion of the environments;
2. A variation of the noise concept. In particular, noise is not only the external sound people hear during a conversation, but also a psychological noise due to natural human factors such as illness, lack of interest and concentration, etc.

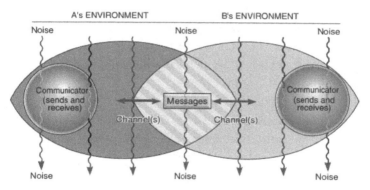

Source: Adler & Proctor II, 2012

Figure 5 - Transactional Communication Model

2.2 The Power of Social Media

The power and importance of SM is growing because more and more people are using them and making them an important part of their daily life. In particular, this situation is happening because:

1. There is an increase of the **Internet access opportunities** due to:
   a. A wide variety of options for the Internet connection (e.g. mobile devices and desktops);
   b. Increase of the world's population, meaning more users joining SM;
   c. Increase of necessity and increase of business needs (e.g. communication, information and ecommerce);
   d. More opportunities to use the Internet due to free Wi-Fi connections (i.e. in recreational or business areas).

2. Change of **societal habits and demography**. Today's generation, born in the SM era, is replacing the older one who is more familiar with traditional media such as:

   a) Broadcast media (i.e. TV and radio). They have the main characteristic of reaching a large audience but have also difficulties in targeting specific groups of people with common needs.
   b) Print media (e.g. newspapers and magazines). They reach a smaller audience but with shared interests or characteristics (e.g. specific magazine for hobbies and interests). This media base their success on the interest met in the community regarding the programming and for the size of the geographic area covered by distribution.
   c) One to one communication (e.g. letters, newsletters and postcards). They have a high level of targeting but they are also expensive. If this method is used by companies and the response's

number of the recipient is low, this method can be very expensive.

Besides the popular factors analysed in Chapter One, SM also have **key characteristics** that make them popular in spotlight and that are crucial for their success. In fact, they are considered to be:

1. Vehicles for the **fast circulation of information.** The information is not just shared between two people but it can be spread from one to another or to an entire virtual community, as happened during the *"Arab Revolution"* in 2011, the *"Occupy Wall Street"* protest in 2011, or the Brazilian protest *"Vem pra rua"* ("come to the street") in 2013.

2. **Sources of news.** Ordinary people can become news generators if they want to, and this phenomenon increases the amount of news in circulation. For example, posting a: photo, message or article can teach the reader something or give more information about a situation or status, such as the birth of child, from a friend, or the launch of a new product from a company.

3. **Two-way interactions.** Users do not just acquire information but they can also comment, reply directly to the sender and share it publicly. This makes the "sender" and the "receiver" at equal levels of interaction. For example, users have the ability to: comment on an article and, potentially, benefit from the same article's audience; complain about a service disruption or a bad experience with some products they have used; inform other users about scams; interact with people they admire or support (e.g. a favourite football player, politician or journalist).

4. **Availability of the media.** The platforms are potentially available at anytime and anywhere (potentially because they depend to the Internet connection). For example, people can post or comment on pictures during events like holidays, weddings or sports events. Moreover, they can send emails or download documents while they are in a taxi.

5. **Accurate Databases.** Some SM are self-updated databases. Indeed, they store users' critical information, such as employment status, location, friendship network, political and religious views, siblings' name, personal pictures and videos. It is also true that in some cases users create fake accounts or leave some information blank, but, overall, SM are reliable sources of personal information compared to other databases built in the traditional way. In addition, they make research of people or groups of interests easier.

2.3 How Social Media Affect Interpersonal Communication

Nowadays, most of people consider SM as part of their daily life and routine but, despite all the good and valid characteristics analysed in the previous section, SM also have weaknesses. If I had to compare them with the traditional face-to-face communication method, these weaknesses would become more evident because the lack of:

1. Facial and gestural expressions;
2. Touch;
3. Sounds;
4. Perceptions.

The mix of the characteristics and senses in the above list has been the basis of human communication but the use of SM means new challenges due to the utilization of hardware devices.

SM users create their personalities and maintain their credibility using specific skills and behaviour based on writing and posting images, videos or emotion icons.

Among SM, only video calling applications are very close to traditional communication methods, because they can mitigate the weaknesses of the previous list.

According to Auvinen (2012), SM have influenced eight important changes in communication, which I define and summarise below:

1. **Anonymity.** Users have the possibility to use nicknames or aliases and not take responsibility for their statements, comments or questions.
2. **Plurality of information sources.** SM can provide unprecedented plurality of opinion and information from generic or specialized sources, apart the traditional ones (e.g. newspapers and magazines).
3. **Omnipresence.** SM are vehicles for news generators, which can be developed and spread in any circumstance and anywhere as long as there is access to the SM device. Public and private lives of individuals have merged and potentially any private discussion or opinion can be revealed to the public by anyone.
4. **Fast circulation of information.** The information sent out travels quickly throughout the virtual community supported also by mobile technology.
5. **Equality** for users. They are at same level of communication with each other and there is not

hierarchy between them. For example, anybody can post, tweet or send content that can be replied or commented by the "receiver".

6. **Subjectivity.** Users provide own view on event and they report news acquired by personal experience. Because these multiple and personal opinions on SM, readers can easily get false information and believe in it.

7. **Flexible media.** These new media are a combination of multiple digital contents and format (e.g. video, text, audio and animation).

8. **Difficult to control by regulator.** This situation is due to the fact that SM are relatively new methods of communication and in constant evolution. Valid specialists can bypass any control or censure and spread information.

Due to the characteristics listed above, SM have a well-established role in today's communication and they have also influenced the ways and habits of communication. Indeed, users' discussions tend to be:

a) **Continuous.** Because users never virtually separate from others and a dialogue can last as long as they like.

b) **Effective & Concise.** The use of devices forces us to be concise and go straight to the point. SM make it easier to reach the people we need or with the characteristics we like (in case we are establishing new relationships or we are finding old friends that we are not currently in touch with).

c) **Global.** There is the possibility to reach and interact with people around the world. This characteristic gives more opportunities to those who want to benefit from an extended economic market.

In summary, keeping in mind the points above, senders and receivers follow an implicit protocol of communication. The messages, comments and posts tend to be short and concise; these can be sent and red potentially by anyone in the world and, because of the brevity of the messages, the senders go straight to the point.

This means that SM favour the increase of number of interactions, which are made by shorter sentences than other media.

SM give the possibility to anyone, with access to the Internet, to create the news and to spread it around the world. They can use a simple tweet or post something on YouTube for example.

People use SM with different modalities and I have grouped them based on the following main traits:

a) *Active,* who likes to populate SM with content: posting material, commenting, sending friend invitations, creating and managing forums, etc.
b) *Neutral,* who participate as an observer and doesn't like to be involved or leave a trace.
c) *Reactive,* who uses and works on existing content, e.g. responding to messages, posting comments on other subjects, etc.

As I said above, people use the three modalities at different times and with different mixes, but they tend to be prevalent in one in particular. They approach SM as they approach communication in real life, i.e. there is the talker, the listener, and the one who acts only if stimulated.

2.3.1 Language and Behaviour

There are also other changes due to the use of SM, indeed they affect language and human behaviour. In particular:

1. **Language** is adapting to this new media: skipping the formality and arriving to the essence of the message. Even the message length is reduced to be quick. Words like Facebook became fb; Regarding, Re; Thanks, Thx; Kisses, XX.

2. **Human** behaviour. Users can:

   a) Develop and benefit of multitasking and mobility. SM have been developed to be used anywhere and anytime with the scope to meet business needs and societal transformations. For example, it is a common habits waiting at bus stop and also checking at same time SN or the current bus location through App. Moreover, walking and check for new tweets; text somebody and talking to somebody else at the same time.

   b) Develop the tendency of a temporary and "unique" isolation because also absorbed by a virtual life. The classic example is the group of people when members, even only for a short moment, are too busy replying to emails, texting, posting photos, watching videos or tweeting.

Source: Fadek, 2011

Figure 6 – Communication in the SM age

Research in mobile technology has accomplished many important achievements. Only a few years ago, online chat was only possible on desktops, indeed mobile phones were only used for making calls. When the texting feature was invented, it represented a big achievement and changed the telephony market. Since then, the mobile phones innovations never stopped: better format, lighter, touch screen, and connected to the Internet of course. This last feature made the mobile phones more appealing. Indeed, the Internet provides information, localises mobile devices (and the user), and makes software applications more useful.

The evolution of society is also based on communication and usually people use the most advanced technology available for this. For example, letters, books, newspapers and even smoke signals were used for centuries to communicate. In general, newer and faster communications technologies are developed when either one of the factors below happens:

1. Society becomes more complex to be supported with the same technology. This means the current methods of communication do not satisfy anymore society's

needs (e.g. business, entertainment and social interaction) due to the increase of the number of interactions and the quality required. For example, people want communicate quicker, at any time and to exchange the widest variety of data type possible.

2. Research & Development. These make new technology available and affordable due to discoveries and optimization of the existing ones. This can attract people interest and develop new trends. For example, electronic money funds, mobile phones, space flight, personal computers, etc.

In communication, technology progress aims to reach more people and to reduce the time to connect with others.

2.4 Social Media and Traditional Media

As seen in the previous section, SM have an important role in communication and they have differences with traditional media (TM).

The role of both media categories is identical, such as: inform, educate and influence opinion but, as shown in Tab.1, they approach and send messages to the audience in different ways. Indeed, the table highlights some important differences between the two media categories. The comparison tells us that SM are versatile, in contrast with the static and "top- down" working principle of TM.

Furthermore, SM are described as democratic media because the cost for accessing them is lower than TM (poorer people have the possibility to get and generate information) and also because they support and favor democratic behaviors, such as:

a) "Citizen journalism" (based upon the idea that potentially every citizen can collect, report and spread the information);

b) Interactions between peers based on: news, idea and information.

Table 1 – Social Media compared with Traditional Media

SOCIAL MEDIA COMMUNICATION	TRADITIONAL MEDIA COMMUNICATION
Internet and mobile means of communication	Traditional means of communication: i.e. Television, radio, newspapers and magazines.
Engaging people and audience	Informing people and audience
Unstructured sharing of information	Structured sharing of information
Two way communication (dialogue)	One way communication (monologue)
Quick and instant information dissemination	Bound to fixed schedules, press deadlines
Talking to Customers/Consumers	Talking at Customers/Consumers
Public Audience exercise control on the flow of information	Government/Businesses/ Organizations exercise control on the flow of information
Decentralized information distribution process	Centralized information distribution process
Consumer sponsored communication	Organization sponsored communication
Fuelled by internet research, peers and friends opinions, preferences and recommendations	Fueled by organization's advertising/marketing campaigns
Trustworthy and transparent	Speculates and lacks transparency
Fosters Citizen Journalism	No public involvement
Potentially dangerous as it can easily lead to rumors/gossip mongering	"Gatekeepers" prohibit irrelevant and false information
Practical, easy and inexpensive	Unpractical, complicated and expensive
Easy updatable & immediately	Fixed, unalterable
Instant popularity gauge	Professional Content
Archives are easy to access	Archives are cumbersome to access
All media can be mixed	Limited Media mix
Individual publishers	Commissioned publishers
Easily backed up & stored	Vulnerable to loss or damage

Source: Laad & Lewis, 2012

In 2013, during my stay in New York, I watched a news program because attracted by the topic of discussion. It was about the differences between traditional media and social media, well the TM experts repeated twice the concept that a massive use of SM would reduce the quality and the variety of information received by people because users focalise only on what they are interested, overlooking the rest of the news. They talked about the trend of both audience and readers as thermometer of interest in TM but they never mentioned or analysed the quality of the information provided by TM compared to SM.

I understand that both experts and anchorman have been working for the TM industry but the times have changed and new media are available for the society and people have to deal with them.

In the era of SM, news does not exclusively fall from national broadcasters on people because there is also the possibility for people of collecting, reporting and spreading the information as well (as seen above in this section).

I agree that there is the risk for users to focalise only on specific arguments but SM represent some of the different sources available today for acquiring information. Furthermore, these media offer the possibility also to traditional broadcaster to use them for reaching audience.

2.4.1 Analysis of Traditional Media

The development, and expansion, of SM puts pressure on the entire TM industry because their users' demands have changed and now they start to embrace SM.

As reported in the previous section, TM cannot support and satisfy all the needs of the society due to their intrinsic characteristics. In specific:

1. **Television**. It combines sound, image and story representations. It is the mass media per excellence and it is capable of highly influencing public opinion and of selling itself as a credible source of information. Because of this central role and importance, and because it is completely opposite in nature to SM, this medium is the one that suffers most from SM's development.

2. **Radio**. This medium is able to reach an audience in multiple places and during different activities (e.g. while driving, working, exercising, eating and talking). Compared to TV, radio has a reduced audience, but on the other hand, it develops loyal listeners and it has the ability to modify itself, and quickly add or eliminate content.

3. **Print**. This medium is different from the others because it posts high-quality images and focuses on specific topics argumentation. It has a limited circulation due to the high cost of distribution. The content and the analysis offered to the reader, however, still make it interesting. Print is the medium that can most easily adapt and benefit from integration with SM because it can reduce distribution costs and increase the number of readers.

Usually, when a new medium is available for the public audience, the older ones transform themselves in order to be competitive. For example, current newspapers are different from the ones printed before the arrival of TV in the families. In particular, TV was quickly accepted by people due to images, sounds and the high level of entertainment for the viewer. Newspapers responded with more colours and images on their printed copies to stay competitive. Print tried also to differentiate their output with greater specialization, scientific analyses and reports.

Fig. 7 shows the device penetration in the population and according to Global Web Index (2015), there is a large usage of online content and TV represents still the main medium among TM. Users spend almost six hours on the internet (the study reveals that the combination of PC, Tablet and Laptop usage is higher than mobile phone). There is a clear lower interest for Radio, Press and Gaming and the report includes also online access for TV, Radio and Press.

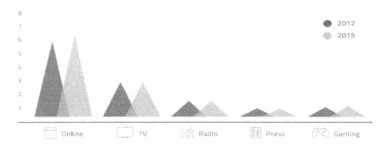

Source GlobalWebIndex, 2015

Figure 7 - Media Consumption Behaviors by Medium: 2012 Vs 2015.

SM are also a platform, which can assimilate TM and allow these to stay competitive. Specifically for TM, the study of Global Web Index inform about the time spent on online TM and SN for the range of age (see Fig.8). Probably does not surprise to find out that people (in particular teens) spend more time with SNs rather than online TV, which still remain the second media of interest of this special rank.

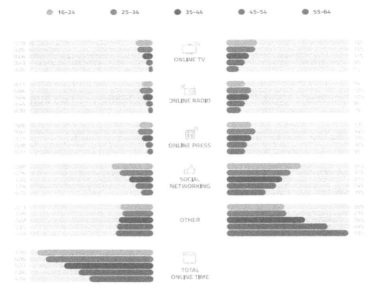

Source GlobalWebIndex, 2015

Figure 8 - Media Consumption Behaviors by ages

According to Innis (2008), media comes in two forms: **time-biased** and **space-biased,** and both are important elements to progress civilization.

Time-biased media are the ones that more than the others are able to carry a message for generations, such as: clay or stone tablets, oral sources like Homer's epic poem, hand-copied manuscripts on parchment or vellum. As can be imaged, this type reaches only a limited number of people and they facilitate religion, stability, community and tradition.

In contrast, **space-biased** media cover longer distances, but with fleeting content. TM are part of this category, indeed radio, TV and newspapers have these characteristics and, very importantly, they favour: empire expansion and conservation, rapid changes of systems, secularism and materialism.

The author maintains that a society, which emphasizes time-biased media, uses objects with a durable character like clay or stone because they have to preserve the history, song and tradition, and must pass the message unchanged to the next generation. For these characteristics, the time-biased media favour decentralization and a hierarchy-style of social organization. In particular, societies with a media system based exclusively on time-biased are hierarchical and, in some, cases they use consensus to operate. They use memory to pass the tradition and uses, rely on older people's experiences and favour concrete thinking versus abstract.

In contrast, societies who emphasize space-biased media use materials that are less durable in character for example paper, favour trade and administration, and are very easy to modify. Furthermore, they favour an abstract approach over the concrete. For these societies, tradition is not the primary importance, and their way of thinking appears rational, linear and impersonal.

Innis (1950), also analyses the influence of media in ancient empires. He maintained that societies based on light and easy transport forms of communication (like papyrus) have a good political and administrative control of the space. This is because the medium they use facilitates the transmission of the message over long distances and because they target, very well, the receivers (audience). For example, the predominant medium of the Roman Empire was the papyrus, which was also part of the reason for the long existence of this Empire. After the collapse, parchment became the most used medium, and the author believes that this medium favours a decentralized form of social organization because it is a durable medium used for manuscripts in medieval monasteries. This means that parchment is an expression of religious control of information over the time and for this reason it is associated with time-biased media.

Innis highlights that the two types of media have different scopes; from one side a time-biased medium is orientated to preserve a local culture over time, on the other side the space-biased medium spreads the influence of a culture over distance.

The author suggests that empires survive only if they find the right balance between the two media; indeed, when a second media is introduced to the society where only one type of media is predominant, this will stress the bias of the first one and enrich the society with more characteristics and better analysis. Innis supports this idea by using the example of the Byzantine Empire, where both papyrus (which supported political control and was typical of space-biased media) and parchment (typical of time-biased media and used by ecclesiastic organizations) were used to benefit the local community and the entire empire's structure.

Furthermore, in the time of Plato, Ancient Greece had expanded its influence over Europe because a written communication became popular among philosophers and government organisations; together with the prominent verbal communication. Indeed, Plato tried to adapt the new medium of prose to Socrates' dialogue (Socrates was one of the greatest exponents of the oral tradition) and from the following scripts, Plato was able to formulate new philosophical concepts. When writing became more prevalent and Ancient Greece's balance was upset, a new empire rose up; this was the Roman Empire because based most of all on written communication also because the large availability of papyrus.

Based on the elements shown in this section, I place SM belong in the category of space-biased media. These new media push the axis of communication in contemporary society towards the space-biased category and put pressure on the role of TM.

If a second media is introduced to a community, and over time acquires more influence than the first ones (due to the increased use of them), this leads to a change in the society, providing unique traits to it. Some big changes are discussed in the next chapter, such as the case of the Arab revolutions, the election of new presidents, or the new way of doing economics.

As happened in past empires, in order to predict which countries will benefit from the use of SM it must be analysed today which countries have the technology to support SM, which ones gain any benefit from the use of them, and which ones can control these media, which represent tools of new social and cultural expression.

2.5 Market opportunity and Users profile

As I reported, SM are a consequence of the Internet development and the growing usage is supported, in particular, by **mobile technology and Apps** useful for people and companies. These last two things are important because they make SM appreciated and available anytime, anywhere and for any occasion (e.g. push a button to get a cab in the desired location, publish images on a favourite SN, or communicate with somebody for work or pleasure). In this section, I present an overview of what these new media represents nowadays.

In specific, the countries with high penetration (>45%) of the Internet in 2014 and with highest number of users are: China, USA and Japan (see Tab. 2). Despite the number of inhabitants, and sorting the table by population penetration, the ranking is different because the main countries become: UK, Canada/Japan and Republic of Korea.

Table 2 - Countries with Internet Penetration >45%, 2014

Rank	Country	2014 Internet Users (MM)	2014 Internet User Growth	2013 Internet User Growth	Population Penetration	Total Population (MM)	Per Cap GDP ($0
1	China	632	7%	10%	47%	1,356	$13
2	United States	269	2	2	84	319	$55
3	Japan	110	0	9	86	127	$37
4	Brazil	105	4	12	52	203	$16
5	Russia	87	15	9	61	142	$25
6	Germany	68	0	1	84	81	$46
7	United Kingdom	57	4	1	90	64	$40
8	France	54	-1	5	82	66	$40
9	Iran (I.R.)	49	8	16	60	81	$17
10	Egypt	43	15	13	50	87	$11
11	Korea (Rep.)	42	1	1	85	49	$35
12	Turkey	38	4	6	46	82	$20
13	Italy	36	1	2	58	62	$35
14	Spain	34	0	7	72	48	$34
15	Canada	30	0	5	86	35	$45
	Top 15	1,653	5%	7%	59%	2,800	
	World	2,793	8%	10%	39%	7,176	

Source Meeker (2015)

Regarding the smartphones penetration, the study reveals that USA, Japan and Brazil are the biggest in terms of number of existent users but if we apply the same sorting criteria as in the previous analysis, the highest penetration if for Australia (100%) followed by Saudi Arabia and Japan.

Table 3 - Smartphone Markets with >45% Penetration

Rank	Country	2014 Smartphone Subs (MM)	2014 Smartphone Sub Growth	2013 Smartphone Sub Growth	Population Penetration	Total Population (MM)	Per Capita GDP ($000)
1	USA	204	9%	16%	64%	319	$55
2	Japan	104	5	5	82	127	$37
3	Brazil	96	28	43	47	203	$16
4	Germany	52	33	30	65	81	$46
5	United Kingdom	45	9	14	71	64	$40
6	France	43	16	43	65	66	$40
7	South Korea	39	5	15	80	49	$35
8	Spain	26	1	19	55	48	$34
9	Saudi Arabia	25	14	6	91	27	$52
10	South Africa	23	26	48	47	48	$13
11	Australia	22	1	40	100	23	$46
12	Canada	21	16	20	60	35	$45
13	Argentina	20	28	52	47	43	$23
14	Malaysia	20	16	38	66	30	$25
15	Taiwan	14	1	50	61	23	$46
	Top 15	756	13%	21%	64%	1,186	
	World	2,107	23%	27%	29%	7,176	

Source Meeker (2015)

Comparing the two tables emerges that for the top 15 countries, the smartphone device has a higher penetration than the Internet one (if we consider the top 15 Countries) but this conclusion is inverted for the World devices penetration.

If we focus on USA, which is one of the biggest markets for number of users in the world, a recent study on Social Media (Perrin, 2015) gives an overview on SM usage trends and refine the main traits of the users. In particular, the study reveals that:

- The 90% of **young adults** (ages 18 to 29) are the most likely to use social media; the second position is for middle aged (30-49) with a 77% and then mature people (50-64) with a 51%. The study found out also a significant increase of SM use for seniors (over 65 years old), indeed they reached the 35% compared to 27% in 2014.
- **Genders.** Men and woman have the same attitude, with no major differences.
- **Higher income** households (75K+) and with a **college** (o more) degree use more SM than others categories.
- **Suburban residents** have passed the number of urban residents; now, they lead the statistics with the 68% of them use SM versus a 64% of urban ones. Rural residents follow with a 58%.

Nielsen (2014) has also released a study, which lists the main typical places where Americans use SM and the main common characteristic for the users. In specific:

1. **In Car.** The 31% of Americans use SM in car and the 48% of them are moms with kids under 13 years old.
2. **Office**. The 39% of Americans use SM while at work. In specific, 56% are adults (25-34) and the 57% are wealthier households (income $150k+).
3. **Restaurant.** The 31% of Americans use SM around a table of which the 44% are young adults (25-34).
4. **Bathroom.** The 21% of Americans use SM in bathroom and the young adult (18-24) are the 40%.

From a business point of view, companies have included or focused their business interests on this new digital media, and they have been stimulating the media market with advertisements and innovations. This fresh flow of investment in SM combined with the consumer interest, encourage entrepreneurs, and big corporations, to invest in SM projects.

According to largest statistics portal Statista (2015), the worldwide revenue forecast generated by consumers for mobile apps via stores, will have a big increase in 2020. This revenue will generate $100 B and this represents one of the biggest cash markets for companies. Focusing on USA media markets, Meeker (2015) reports that in 2014 the majority of people spent time watching TV, followed by the Internet and Mobile (with a positive growing trend). Most of money spent for Ads went to TV, the Internet and Print. Among the entire media industry, Mobile is the one very compelling with a high Y/Y growing rate of users and very low investment in Ads that gives a better cost-benefit ratio for those who use this channel for advertisements. Fig. 10 shows this situation and the arrows represent the Y/Y change.

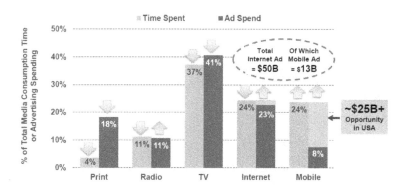

Source: Meeker, 2015

Figure 9 – Relation between % time spent in media vs. % of advertising spending (USA, 2014)

For the companies, they also realised that SM give the possibility to know better their audience and target this more effectively and find and expand their new and existing business. Compared to the traditional media, whose messages are "untouchable" by the audience, SM allow the capture of instant customers' feedbacks and information. Furthermore, companies believe that SM can help them to reduce costs for business generation and brand awareness.

Chapter Three

Impact on People's Lives

Nowadays, social media are a reality and they are becoming more and more important and central to daily life, motivated by business and personal interests. The growth of SM's importance also implies a development of intrinsic power and, in some situations, SM contributes to accomplishing goals in business and personal life. To evaluate the impact on people's lives, this chapter will analyse the influence of SM in three major areas:

1. Politic;
2. Business;
3. Society.

This chapter report practical examples of past and current uses of SM that have changed the World and analyses what SM really represent for the individuals.

3.1 Are Social Media for Everyone?

There is a Latin proverb that says *"Verba volant, scripta manent"*, which means "Spoken words fly away, written words remain".

This proverb should always be in mind when using SM, because whatever is shared, posted or stored on the Internet, will remain forever. In fact, the Internet does not forget and does not lose anything.

With this statement I want to underline that when a message is sent or an opinion or comment is released or posted, nobody can forbid the "receivers" from saving a copy for their purposes, and the senders should expect that their content can be kept and used against them in due time.

SM is an easy and quick way to multiply personal connections for three main reasons: business, entertainment and information.

The entirety of SM is regulated by common sense and by few legal rules; they favour the freedom of expression (almost in democratic countries) and there are almost non-existent limits to use these media.

I also suggest looking at SM as one big database, where personal information circulate and are stored (e.g. in a social network, in the cloud or in web chats). The main characteristic of this big database is that it is self-updated and self-powered, and can be a megaphone of a person's life. This can also bring about negative consequences, as analysed later in this book.

If I had to define SM system with one word, I would say that it is a set of tools (with the characteristics described in section two) and tools do not harm anyone if the user knows how to use them. To be more specific, they are tools for today's communication, and if they are used with a lack of care, or for unlawful activities, they can hurt somebody else or the users themselves.

People should also not be afraid of this new media. For example, I hear many parents saying that they need to control their kids' social networks, I believe that the priority is to educate the kids how use SM and how defend from possible threats coming from them. In this way it is possible to prevent possible problems and make them understand the risks.

Somebody also asked me if there should be some limitation to SM by law, such as an independent organisation to control our chats, emails, postings, videos, identity, etc. But don't we have already a clear law that protects us from illicit, harmful and illegal actions? Does a massive and extended privacy restriction really help and, besides, who and what will be the right organisation or individual to control the controllers? In general, restrictions have never made a society evolve.

3.2 Political impact

In the last few years we have seen many revolutions or revolts that were started, organised and documented using SM. There have also been situations when political campaigns involved SM to win the elections and when SM influenced public opinion and changed human behaviour.

One of the major cases was the "Arab Spring". In 2011, the Islamic world faced a big political change. Countries such as Tunisia, Libya, Egypt, Syria, and Bahrain were in revolt. People fought against their government for more democracy and freedom. Anyone in the world with the Internet connection could watch the live images coming from those countries in revolt via Facebook, web streaming or YouTube.

In contrast to the past years, when information was processed and spread by traditional media, nowadays any news can be reported by anyone, and broadcast in real time. Users decide if the information is relevant or not, interesting or not and, in this case, can choose to share it with their followers, and so the process repeats itself.

The following sub-paragraphs report some famous cases around the world where SM were essential for the creation and development of the events.

3.2.1 Philippines
In October 2000, the former President J. Estrada was in middle of a corruption scandal. In January 2001, it escalated to a people's protest. This happened when a dedicated court, assigned to the impeachment, forbade opening an envelope containing possible evidence of the President's involvement in the scandal. The Court stated that this evidence was not part of the impeachment process and this means that it should not be taken in consideration.

In few hours, hundreds of thousands of angry text messages circulated among the population against the verdict. People flooded the streets of Manila becoming a serious threat to the security of the nation. After three days of protests, the military took the side of the population and Estrada had to resign from presidency.

This was the first important episode involving SM that affected an important political resolution. In those circumstances, SM was able to highlight a judicial court decision that was wrong for the population, which then organised a revolt.

3.2.2 Tunisia
In December 2010, a Tunisian street vendor, **Tarek al-Tayeb Mohamed Bouazizi,** publicly immolated himself in protest of municipal officials abusing their position. By coincidence, the

event was recorded on video, which was then uploaded and watched by many people in following days.

Bouazizi's action, summarised and spread by this cruel video, represented the start of the Tunisian revolution and the *"Arab Spring"* protest in general. The protesters were people that felt to be in the same situation as Bouazizi; they demanded justice for him and to improve the social and political situation of Tunisia.

To limit the protesters' actions, the government tried to block YouTube and the Internet access in general, but, because this was not entirely restricted, the protesters' technology experts bypassed the blockage using different techniques. They were able to keep a link established between the protesters and the major news corporations and to maintain the flow of information from the inside country to the worldwide public.

In Tunisia, the Internet is a well-established and used system of communication and, according to Freedom House (2012), in 2011 the Internet penetration was only 39% for a population of 10.8 m.

With Bouazizi's death, after few days before the beginning of the protest, the fights intensified and President **Zine El Abidine Ben Ali** was obliged to resign. He was in power for twenty years and the people saw in him all the worst of the country.

3.2.3 Egypt
The epilogue of the revolt in Tunisia, became one of the triggers of other revolts in Islamic countries.

In January 2011, **Egypt** saw a wave of protests from its population for better living conditions. Protesters were part of different socio-economic and religious classes. They fought against police brutality, corruption, unemployment, lack of free elections, food inflation, etc.

On this occasion, SM also played an important role in the events that led to the revolution. **Khaled Mohamed Saeed** was a young Egyptian man that was beaten to death by local police after he had been arrested in a cybercafé. Both the post-mortem images of Khaled and the cruel event publicly revealed by the cybercafé owner and other witnesses, caused public resentment. As sign of protest, the computer engineer Wael Ghonim, opened a Facebook page entitled "We are all Khaled Saeed". In few days, hundreds of thousands people joined the page, which had a picture of Saeed dead on the front page . Due to this huge support, the clear evidence of police involvement and the international criticism for the incident, the Egyptian government sent to trial the police officers involved in the homicide.

This was not sufficient for the protestors, who demanded an increase in their quality of life. Protestors flooded Cairo's streets for a big demonstration, also gaining the support of the military, which they claimed they would not intervene against the rebels in any way.

The protesters' objectives were peaceful demonstration and civil disobedience. The government tried to block the protest by censoring Facebook, Twitter and restricting the use of the Internet. This was a bad decision because it caused financial damages to companies that used the Internet for their core business and because the protestors gained more support from the world's public opinion, finding foreign allies among the Internet specialist groups, which helped them to bypass the Internet censorship. After two weeks of riots and foreign pressure, President Mubarak resigned, marking the end of 31 years of state emergency. Moreover, the State Security

Investigations Service was disbanded and the NDP was dissolved.

A new democratic President was elected and a new Constitution was approved.

In recognition of these events, *"Time"* magazine included Mr Wael Ghonim in the 100 most influential people for the year 2011 (El Baradei, 2011). In his article, El Baradei stated that Mr Ghonim was to be praised because he contributed to the start of the peaceful revolution.

In the three circumstances described above, SM created a sense of awareness in the population, revealing the poor quality of their life. The protests achieved their goals because of the participation of a large number of the population, the poor social and economic situations, and the shocking and cruel homicide.

3.2.3 Italy

In **Italy**, the political "5 Stars Movement" (M5S), was conceived to communicate and interact with the population by using SM exclusively. The movement's creators, Casaleggio and Grillo, believed that SM is ideal for politics. In particular, the two founders, highlighted that SM:

1. "Store" on the Internet the promises made by candidates. This motivates candidates to accomplish their goals during their mandate.
2. Favour the transparency of politicians because the personal background could easily come out and, furthermore, the political decisions are monitored and easily commented by users. This means that candidates have all the interest to provide correct

information and follow up the promises made during the political campaign.

3. Favour cost reductions because it is much cheaper than traditional media for the political campaign and ongoing political activities.
4. Favour two-way communication. Indeed, the electorate can also comment or give indications and feedback directly to politicians.
5. Favour democracy, because no elector is excluded and potentially anyone can propose solutions for a communal problem, provide opinions or comment on political decisions.

The movement was founded during a time of distrust of politics also as consequence of the economic crisis and it is based on a few main ideas, such as: transparency (decisions must be shared on the Internet and with the electorate), e-democracy, no public funds for political parties, environment preservation, and eco-friendly production.

In addition to the usage of SM, specifically Twitter, Facebook and YouTube, the M5S also uses public speech in city squares to communicate during political campaigns.

The communication methods and the movement's innovative ideas, pleased the SM generation very much, to the point they voted for the party, allowing the M5S to gain seats in the Italian Parliament just few years after its creation.

Indeed, M5S was created on 4th of October 2009 and, according to the parliamentary results in 2013 (ilsole24ore, 2013), it was elected as first party in Lower House and second party in the Upper House.

According to the Archive of Political Elections (Ministero dell'Interno, 2013), since its creation M5S had the following results:

- 2010: 4 Councillors and 8 City Councillors.
- 2011: 34 City Councillors elected in 28 Councils.
- 2012: 4 Mayors (Castiglion, Pizzarotti, Fabbri, and Maniero) and it is the first party in Sicily, with 14.88% of the vote.
- 2013: 109 MPs in the Lower House and 54 MPs in Upper House.
- 2014: they got the 21% of the vote for the European Parliament, getting 17 members.

3.2.4 USA

In 2008, **Barack Obama** achieved an extraordinary election success by using also SM during his campaign. Indeed, Fig. 11 shows the importance of the Internet among the communications media during the campaign in 2008, and its greater importance in 2012. In particular, between these two years, for the electorate the Internet had the same importance of newspaper and in 2012 it surpassed all others, apart the television. SM gave Obama the ability to spread his political views and to get closer to the constituents, and to the younger generation in particular. He appointed himself as the right President for the right economic and societal change with the motto "Yes, you can", and started asking for small donations for his campaign to reduce his dependence on large ones from big corporations.

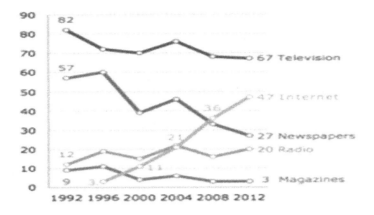

Source: Pew Research Center, 2012

Figure 10 - Internet grows as campaign news source

In 2012, with the use of this new and democratic media, Obama gave an example of political change. The majority of voters supported Obama because they felt he would make a difference, stimulate good national change, and because they felt close to him, like he was "one of them".

At the same time, his opponent Mitt Romney faced difficult times. On YouTube, for example, there are videos leaked where apparently he said things that upset many electors.

For Romney, SM had a different result; just using SM does not guarantee the success.

3.3 Marketing impact

This section reports an SM analysis made for both consumers and sellers. In particular, it analyses how SM have affected the consumer decision-making process and companies' business.

As I reported in the previous chapters, companies and consumers cannot underestimate the influence of SM. For people, can be difficult to realize how deep and extensive SM usage is in today's society but they can understand SM's role for shopping and purchase process.

In 2013, Nielsen released a report on SM which stated that the amount of SM access, using smartphones and tablets, is increasing and it is catching up with the number of users that gain access to SM using a PC (Fig.12). In brief, this means that access to SM can be anytime and anywhere.

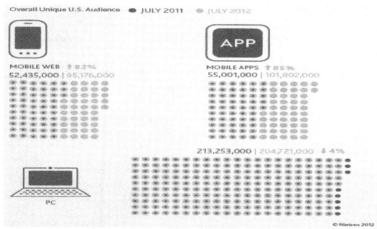

Source: Nielsen, 2012
Figure 11- Number of users per SM device type (USA, 2012)

The time spent on SM has also increased year on year (see Fig. 13).

The figure below shows the time spent on SM using smartphones, tablets and PCs in hours and minutes (HH:MM):

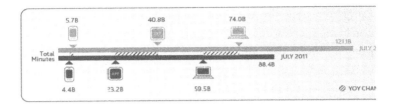

Source: Nielsen, 2012

Figure 12- Time spent on SM devices

The study reports that the number of SM sites is booming and, apart from Facebook and Twitter, many others are experiencing an increase in the number of users (e.g. Pinterest).

The following two sections below highlight two main points:

1. **Purchase decisions** are still individual, but they are influenced by other users' feedback.

2. **Companies** do their best to please their customers in order to get **good reviews.**

3.3.1 Consumer purchase process

On the Internet, there are many stimuli that develop consumer needs. For example, they are generated during or after the reading of: blogs, product or service reviews, and friends' comments or public posts, and in this way SM can influence and alter the **consumer purchase process**.

In particular, SM makes a difference during the ***information search*** period, and also during the ***evaluation of alternatives process***, because the information is quickly found through specialised web pages, videos or social networks. Furthermore, because it is possible to find experts and feedbacks for specific problems and needs, people can evaluate better and more quickly if the need is genuine (this means consumer want to satisfy the need) or just give up. For example, a poor movie review can reduce the desire to watch it, or a product review can stop a potential buyer from purchasing it. As seen in the two previous examples, SM helps buyers to realise that the product or service is not going to improve their lives.

According to Nielsen (2012), during the purchase process, SM are used for different reasons:

a) 70% of those interviewed use it for hearing other's experiences about the product or service in question;

b) 65% of those interviewed use SM to learn more about brands, products and services;

c) 53% of those interviewed use SM for alternatives to brands;

d) 50% use SM to express concerns and make complaints.

The above research has valuable findings on the consumer decision-making journey and is based on a panel survey. This survey was made with 28,000 global consumers with Internet access, and the results showed that SM are able to influence the consumer buying behaviour. In particular, they are very effective for entertainment: 64% of the respondents revealed that they will make a purchase based on a product review. SM are also effective for travel/leisure (60%) and for appliances, food/beverage and clothing/fashion (58%).

3.3.2 Companies

Businesses use a plurality of media for their **marketing campaigns** to boost sales and promote brand image; this section will group the key factors that make SM interesting for companies.

Before the advent of SM, companies promoted their **unique selling proposition** through traditional media. In this way, consumers' objections were handled privately, behind closed doors and using customer service.

With SM, this aspect changed considerably because customer feedback, complaints and opinions cannot be managed in the traditional way, and furthermore these aspects can influence other consumers' decisions. For these two reasons, one of the most valuable elements for companies is their **reputation**. Nowadays, competition is very aggressive for most products and services, and SM spreads consumers' "word of mouth" very easily. This aspect puts under pressure companies' deliverables and increases the quality of customer care.

There are some exceptional examples for using SM to protest against a poor service received, to motivate the company to take action quickly, or to make the public aware about poor company performance. For example, in 2013, Kevin Broadribb uploaded a video to report the poor medical treatment received by his father in Fairfield Hospital in Sydney (Australia), and singer Dave Carroll uploaded his music videos *'United breaks guitars'* to protest against United Airlines, because they refused to pay for guitars after they were broken by baggage handlers.

The use of SM to contact companies' customer care departments is defined as **social care** and, according to Nielsen (2013), it emerged that:

a) 47% SM users utilise social care to interact with a company;

b) Only 1 out 3 SM users prefer to contact the customer care department over the phone, with some differences reported in Fig. 14;

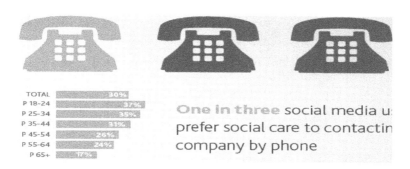

Source: Nielsen 2012

Figure 13- Use of Social Care over the Phone

c) FB was the first SM application used by consumers to deal with the companies' customer services, followed by Twitter and YouTube.

As seen above, on the one hand, customers have the advantage of using SM, on the other hand, companies also benefit. For example, SM **marketing campaigns** are very effective in comparison to more traditional methods. Indeed, mobility is a key characteristic of our current society and most people carry a mobile phone in their pocket and many using social networks. In this way, it is easier for companies to track users' movements and send ads when they are close to specific shops or just to analyse consumers' behaviour to develop personalised marketing campaigns.

Companies track the Internet cookies so that they know the users' interests, and they can adapt their offerings or make people desire specific things.

When users follow a SM group, or they are part of a distribution list, they are open to receiving purchase stimuli from companies (e.g. flight discounts, new model cars, shop discounts and new clothing collections).

The social marketing power that influences the consumer to join communities or groups is defined by J. Turner and R. Shah as social media magnetism.

Social media marketing (SMM), which groups all activities for advertising campaigns, are cheaper than any other alternative and are also very effective in terms of results.

Indeed, SMM is able to:

a) Reach interested customers. For example, showing ads on web pages;

b) Make customers aware of brands. For example, through friends posting, publicity before watching a streaming video or through "likes", which increase brands' visibility.

c) Influence buying decisions. For example, dispelling doubts with good reviews, answering customer questions and through friends' posts. Specifically, Fig. 15 shows the groups of consumers that have purchased goods and services after seeing social ads.

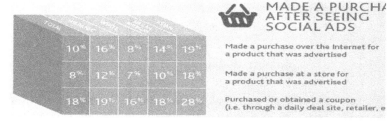

Figure 14- Relationship between Purchase and Social Ads viewing

d) Retain customers. This action is performed, for example, using newsletters, chats and blogs. This means that they are using tools that support customers to answer doubts, clarify situations and solve issues. Customers are also retained with applications able to provide product updates and general information.

There is also the possibility to quantify and compare the contribution of SM in marketing campaigns with the calculation of **Social Return Of Investment** (SROI). This is a rate and originally it was elaborated to monetize extra financial values such as environmental and social value, which impact also the investments made. For the analysis of cost-benefit it is necessary having a marketing plan available, which contains the following four points:

1. **Business goals and objectives and social media campaign objectives**[2].

---

[2] Possible objectives are:
- Increase traffic for blog and website;

2. **SM Strategy.** Based on the objectives identified, the plan requires a short and long strategy of communication. For example, if the need is to increase the number of business leads generated, one of the options is using the "Lead generation card" of Twitter or "Ad campaign" of Facebook. The flip side is that those two activities are effective in the short term and, for a long term plan, for example they need be supported by a blog in order to have leads generated by the own traffic. Instead, if the goal is to boost sales with e-commerce, a short term strategy could include Facebook "carousel ads" and develop Apps for a long term plan, which provide customer with a friendly way to interact and buy from the company.

3. **Traffic analysis.** The analysis of visitors' traffic for the channels used can reveal important information to improve the effectiveness of the campaign itself. It is possible to use applications and services provided by external companies to get a clear picture of the users and to identify prospects and the company messages.

4. **SROI calculation and evaluation.** The formula to calculate the Social Return of Investment is: SROI= (Benefit − costs) x 100 / Costs. After calculating the rate is also important to analyse if the results are in line with plan's objectives. Furthermore, beside the calculation of a mere number, the analysis has to

---

- Increase the number of inbounds calls and consequently the number of business opportunities;
- Increase the online visibility of brand and company's products;
- Establish the reputation among the Social Media community as "Expert" in your topic or market;
- Generate more sales (ecommerce) and improve win rate.

consider also the organisation's social impact generated by the campaign.

3.4 Social Impact

This section analyses the relationship between SM and society to establish a possible link and level of influence that they have on each other.

Nowadays there are many occasions for people to socialise and get to know each other through personal interests and hobbies, workplace and also using SM.

According to the British anthropologist Robin Dunbar (2010), a person can know to 150 people well, because there is no capacity for our minds to keep in touch with a larger number of people. For Dunbar, these 150 connections are trusted and have some emotional link with the subject.

Socialisation requires time to nurture the relationships; for example to get a friend's news, give advice to them, spend quality time with them, congratulate them on their successes, remember their birthday and give the best wishes and exchange presents or favours.

In this scenario, SM can handle part of the effort to stay in touch with others. In particular, software applications do part of the job, for example reminding users about birthdays and events, and also provide the ability to send automatically preloaded standard messages to a user's contacts.

Furthermore, SM are also used to get to know new people and expand connections in addition to methods linked to physical location and face-to-face encounters, such as the workplace, neighbourhood, school, church and clubs.

Like the traditional methods of communication, new media also gives the possibility to create connections based on personal interests and activities, for example, seeking people who like mountain climbing, investing in property, gardening or sporting events.

In this context, the SM expert Adrian Chan (2012) states: *"Social Media are talk technologies"*, arguing also that SM produce outcomes in the age of communication, and they are successful because people are interested in interacting and communicating with others. In addition to that, he considers **interaction and communication** as two important elements of SM, while I genuinely believe that they are SM's **fundamentals**.

Without these two characteristics, SM would lose its appeal, but this can also occur if other two situations happen, which are:

1. The invention of a **new communication system** that makes SM an obsolete technology;
2. **Disinterest** in communication in general, but it is hard to believe today.

From a strictly social perspective, SNs represent the core of SM, and according to Nielsen (2012), people use SNs for different reasons and, as reported in Fig. 16, the popular ones are:

1. Knowing more people in real life through the use of dating applications or searching for experts and specialists to meet.
2. Finding and reaching mutual friends because trusted vehicles of communication, available and intuitive to use.
3. Keeping up with their friends, exchanging opinions or getting updates.

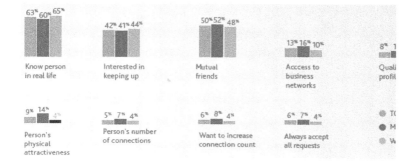

Source: Nielsen 2012

Figure 15 - The Scope of using SN

Furthermore, the survey revealed that 76% of people feel positive after using SNs, 24% feel neutral, and the 21% feel a negative mood.

Regarding the use and scope of SNs, there are six points to consider:

1. SNs increase consumers, because they are a medium used by marketers.
2. SNs are based on collectivism and pluralism concepts. Users join groups, follow profiles and exchange opinions and messages. The purpose could also include personal objectives, but on SNs the number of a group's members and the number of an individual's social connections determine the importance in the network.
3. Making virtual friends or collaborating with remote people (e.g. asking advice and getting information). On the one hand, this is positive because it extends

the range of qualified people it is possible to "meet" (e.g. doctors, engineers, architects and lawyers) and it also reduce the possibility of losing friends because there are opportunities to stay in touch. On the other hand, users have to understand that every action happens remotely, and this means no face-to-face communication or physical letters to send.

4. Asking questions and reading answers in anonymity. This is a powerful benefit if used in an appropriate way (i.e. contacting right people or be in the right community). In this way is possible to get answers for confidential or taboo questions, delicate arguments and problems in the workplace.

5. SNs promote truth and morality because they are transparent, leave a trace of past activities, and other connections can confirm (or not) the background and activities posted. On the Internet, reputation is an important element for doing business or developing connections.

6. Increasing the amount of risk (e.g. being spied on, bullied, robbed and a victim of identity theft) and expose the personal file to critics.

In brief, SM represents a **combination of interactions** using **technology** (i.e. hardware and software applications). They support the spread of ideas, information and decisions almost instantly around the world because they provide a combination of full-time technological platforms (it is possible to use any SM tool at any time) and fast data transmission that make the distance between users unimportant.

Recently I found myself in an interesting conversation, with some colleagues, regarding the possibility of finding true value in friendly relationship developed and maintained only using

SM (as Bauman defines the "on" status). Some colleagues believed that on SM it is possible to find values, develop intimate relationships and trust somebody. I disagreed because SM is just a "vehicle of transportation" for data. People post or share only the things they want to show, highlighting only few good things, for example, and misrepresenting the personal image. Using instant chats, for example, it is very difficult, in some cases, to determine the real mood of the senders or receivers. With this, I want to say that SM are revolutionary, but they cannot replace real life

In brief, SM are a vehicle just like a car, indeed they can be used to transfer things (e.g. messages, data, information and transactions), to keep up with friends and family, to find new connections and to obtain information (e.g. from a bank, car dealer, or travel agency).

3.5 Major Benefits

For how social and business life is organised today, it is very difficult do not use SM. Now more than ever, people's lives have become more interconnected and dependent on large number of connections. Before the Internet boom, life was organised around a few people and possible on the same territory and the face-to–face method of interaction was more important than today. For example, in 90's keeping a friendship going when they lived over 200 km away was a challenge because using the phone was expensive, the car was inconvenient and trains and flights would have taken hours to cover the distance.

SM contributed to changing all of that and establishing and supporting new habits, interests and economic systems like globalisation. For example, new entertainment was developed (e.g. online gaming), the price of transportation has changed (low cost flights and high speed trains), phone calls became cheaper or free (VOIP, Viber, Skype) and broadband was created.

SM also made it possible to find, reach and work with customers located in different countries, and jobs moved to cheaper or more convenient countries, in particular to establish call centres, sales organisations, research and development and administration departments.

SM made it cheaper to travel (e.g. by supporting online booking) because they removed the intermediaries in some cases; they increase in offerings and alternatives for consumers; they also made it easier to purchase any type of service and product (i.e. by using e-commerce). In other words, SM made possible an **effective globalisation** in terms of personal interactions and business.

SM also means **transparency** for any situation, event, and personal background, this means that in theory, SM usage promotes the truth. It is also democratic because anyone (with an Internet connection) can use them and have same condition than others. SM also have two other main advantages:

1. They make users' lives easier. For example, in some cases physical presence is not necessary anymore (e.g. using video conferences, e-votes and online purchases) reducing the stress and expense of travel.
2. They make it easier to research and compare goods, jobs, and services, helping users in their choices.

Chapter Four

Social Media Concerns

Because the popularity of SM is increasing, there are more cases of abuses perpetrated with SM and this chapter focuses on those, listing the major threats and how protect from them.

Among those dangers, there is also the manipulation of user's opinion due to the influence of false proclaims advertised on SM's applications, and the addiction generated by an excessive use of the SM's applications and by the constant use of smart devices, which could generate forms of psychological problems such as anxiety or depression.

4.1 Drawback of Social Media

The common perception is that SM amplify users' actions and make public the personal interests, information and ideas and when these data are shared it is difficult to have them private.

As mentioned in the previous chapters, before start using these new media it is important to understand their characteristics, benefit and risks. In contrast with TM, which are passive media, SM promote users interaction and they support also the expansion of personal connections and this generate more online discussion that can be used by other users eventually.

The following sub-sections are list of common SM dangers and actions that users can take to protect them self.

4.1.1 Opinion Manipulation: Social Media vs. Traditional Media

Social media, like any other media, can be used to alter the reputation of someone or something because, potentially, anyone can post false feedback, stories, or upload fake data and video with the purpose to damage or promote a person, an activity or a company. Furthermore, there is also the risk that uninformed users play into the hands of spiteful people when they share, *like* or approve comments, articles or videos on the Internet and these actions spread false information and could modify the perception of the reality. For example, false information could generate fear and anxiety and influencing a political vote or a purchase decision. SM include different channels of communication and they not protect from opinion manipulation but, on the other side, they provide a multitude users feedbacks and the possibility to reach the original source of news to verify the facts and act accordingly.

It is not avoiding the information that people protect them self from the risk of manipulation but verifying if the source of the information is reliable or not and doing specific research for news of interest, this means evaluate multiple media and multiple sources.

Dishonest people have been using TM for their scopes and the methods they use are sneaky because they deceive audience with false messages.

For example, people could use TM for political success, to keep the power or the status and, in general, for personal profit. For these scopes, TM are used to ridicule an opponent, to alter the perception of the reality and boycott an activity with false statements, or information. The list below reports different strategies used to manipulate public opinion:

a) **Guilt by Association.** Usually, this method shows the picture of an opponent beside an article of lawbreaking or during the report of illegal actions or involves the victim in some shady story even if this is false but only done to confuse the audience.

b) **Verisimilitude.** This strategy makes appear something real when it is not. This is accomplished exaggerating plausible stories and situations or using fantasy characters in real context. The Verisimilitude alter the perception of the reality because the frequency and the vivid actions can make believe that the message is consistent or that it is completely true and people evaluate their life based on that message. There are many examples in movies, cartoons and series TV, such as programs with superheroes, drama series that give the impression that a tropical island is one of the most dangerous places to live for invented crime stories or also programs that show our cities invaded by serial killers, aliens, etc. The verisimilitude is used for different scopes, for example: marketing, education, increase or developing public fears and concerns, improve the public image of subjects, or to create a threat.

c) **Teasing**. This strategy is used for diminishing the opponent's figure, ideas or authority and makes a situation less complicated. In general, this is achieved showing funny pictures of the opponent or doing caricature of the victim.

d) **Sandwich effect**. This strategy uses the medium to show the good of someone and, in between, a weakness. This method is used when the people, who create the news, want to be accepted by the opponent but also leave doubts about the opponent's figure in the audience mind. This strategy is used in particular by newspapers or magazine.

e) **Use of experts**. This method is used, for example, during talk show or during discussion on radio and, in particular, for political, social and business debates. It is a sly way of communication because involves the use of experts for influencing public opinion and both TV programs and presenters are not exposed. In brief, this method includes the selection of experts, which share the same opinion on specific topic and aligned to the program's idea, and invites also a smaller group of experts for the contradictory. The larger group will put pressure on the smaller one during the discussion and this will end, for most of the time, with a victory of the larger group and meeting with the intent of the program.

f) **Character assassination.** An individual has the possibility to use derogatory adjectives to destroy the reputation and credibility of the opponent using exaggeration, false accusation and defamation and many other such as spreading rumors and misinformation.

g) **Message Repetition.** The continuous repetition of a message, through one or more medium, makes the audience believe to the message despite the fact that it can be true or false or useless. For example, this is done to criminalise a politic opposition or a specific group or for marketing purpose. The propaganda uses this method because considered high successful.

h) **Exchange profiles.** This method is used by people with dubious background who want improve their image. They send messages, through TM, to denigrate an opponent and benefit from positive campaign. If this message is constantly repeated and the opponent does not reject the accusation, people start believe it is true.

The above methods are effective when both agenda and communication plan are organised in advance, and when it is used a one-way communication channel, this means they require TM to work properly.

4.1.2 Addictions

Social media can cause dependence, indeed, according to a recent study of University of Chicago (Goessl, 2012), social media is more addictive than cigarettes or alcohol for people. This dependence is revealed through the compulsive check of emails and SN accounts and it is fueled by the large choice of devices available (for the Internet connection) and by the low cost of Internet connection itself.

I want also highlight that SM give to people more reasons and more occasions for using the Web and this continuous access, if not properly controlled, it can entail **the Internet addiction disorder.** This problem is due to the excessive amount of time spent using the Net and this is part of more general technology addiction. For example, a recent online survey (Lookout, 2012) found that the smartphone is an important accessory for people and in particular:

- The 60% of the respondents check the smartphone every hour and young folks, between 18-34 years, are the most addicted (63% of woman and 73% of men);
- The 54% of respondents check the smartphone before sleep, during the night and just after they wake up in the morning.
- The 24% of the respondents check the smartphone while driving.
- The 73% of the respondents felt panicked when they lost their smartphone because the consequent cost & hassle associate with it, bank or financial account exposition and embarrassing photo or text messages present on it.

Apparently, the addiction is generated by the **pleasure** for sharing information publically and also because gives the possibility to **express the personality and creativity**.

"The Week" magazine (Hepburn, 2013) reported the findings of Dr. B.F. Skinner, who conducted an experiment on rats and pigeons. Skinner found out that the unpredictability of the reward is a big motivator for animals. When this reward is predictable, or it comes on irregular base, the animals lose interest but when the reward came at the right time, the brain release endorphins to regulate the pleasure and the animals are motivated.

Some researchers believe that this experiment works well in scenario where people are constantly stimulated by exchange of messages for example text, emails and tweets.

The article also reported the opinion of Dr. Hilarie Cash (Co-founder director of the *"reSTART internet addiction recovery program LLC"*, a rehab program based in Seattle to reduce internet addiction) who states: *"Internet addiction is the same as any other addiction — excessive release of dopamine"*, she also maintains: *"Addiction is addiction. Whether it's gambling, cocaine, alcohol or Facebook"*.

When the mental state cannot detach from the use of the Internet and the online apps, during all day, this can generate insomnia, stress and lack of concentration. In this context, Tim Ferriss (Ferriss, 2011) believes that creativity is suppressed by the overload of activities and checking emails every thirty minutes does not help. The author suggests some actions to protect the individual from mobile phone addiction and allowing the brain to recover. For example, he believes that it is beneficial leaving the mobile phone at home for one day per week, at least; it is manadatory not read emails early in the morning, in order to avoid to set the users in reactive mode; ask the help of collegue or partner to reinforce the will and finally learning the moderation to behave and mitigate the influence of Internet.

4.1.3 Cyber bullying

Cyber bullying is a scourge of modern society that impacts, in most of cases, adolescents and teens and it consists in harassment or bullying another person using the Internet and SM in particular. The phenomenon includes: personal threats, showing hurtful image and videos regarding the victim, identity stealing to hurt or make fun of victim's feelings, share publicly sexting content of the victim with the purpose to damaging the reputation. Usually, cyber bullies act because they believe their action are amusing or to keep their status and power in their community. The victims are targeted for a personal trait, which they cannot correct or modify. The common factors of bullying are: sexual orientation, race, ethnicity and appearance. This phenomenon is alarming and the statics, from National Centre for Social Research (NatCen), describe it also as a growing trend that generates important consequence on victims' mental and physical health.

The researchers Brown, Clery & Fergusson (2011) maintain that the fourth cause of absence from schools is bullying. The survey is based on English students population (i.e. school and home educated), which were absent from school and for which were interviewed their parents.

The research highlights also that the victims of bullying decide to study from home. To be specific, the 18% of the interviewed population fits this category, which is also the first cause for student to have chosen to study from home.

According the National Crime Prevention Council (NCPC) the cyber bullying victims tend to react in two ways:

1. Active mode:
   - Seeking revenge;
   - Cyber bullying back.
2. Passive mode:
   - Avoiding friends and activities;
   - Subject to anxiety;
   - Subject to depression;
   - Subject to suicide (also defined bullycide). This happen in rare and extreme case when victims feel: terrified, offended and embarrassed.

NCPC also provides advices for cyber bullying prevention and to contrast this shameful and anti-social behavior:

1. Refuse to pass along cyber bullying messages;
2. Tell friends to stop cyber bullying;
3. Block communication with cyber bullies;
4. Report cyber bullying to a trusted adult;
5. Never post or share personal information online (this includes full name, address, telephone number, school name, parents' names, credit card number or Social Security number) or friends' personal information;
6. Never share SM passwords with anyone, except own parents;
7. Talk to the parents about online activities.

Families play an important role in the prevention of cyber bullying, when they make children aware about this possible treat, when they make sure that personal information are not public on children's profile and when they make sure their children understand that the role of parents is also protecting them from bullying treats or helping them when this circumstance happens eventually.

According to **Ditch the Label** (Ditch the Label, 2013), it emerges that:

- 7 in 10 young people are victims of cyber bullying;
- The 20% of young people experience extreme cyber bullying on a daily basis;
- Facebook, Ask.FM and Twitter found to be the most likely sources of cyber bullying;

- An estimated 5.43 m young people in the UK have experienced cyber bullying, with 1.26 m subjected to extreme cyber bullying on a daily basis.

The survey was conducted online only, with a sample of 10.008 young people aged between 13 and 22 and with a distribution of: 67% from UK, 17% form USA, 12% from Australia and 4% from different countries.

In particular, the victims admitted that the cyber bullying has an important impact on self-esteem, it affects the social life for quite some time, it decreases the optimism, and it has huge impact on studies performance and future carrier plans. Moreover they face also isolation, anti-social behaviour and loss of appetite.

Cyber bullying creates also problems at home, because the victim does not know how to manage the situation and the consequent anger and frustration pour in the family.

This phenomenon can be contained by different actions, the family has a primary role in this and a common sense approach is valid in any situation. It is important for parents establishing a trustworthy and understanding relationship with their children, which need to know that they can rely on them and ask for anything without fear or embarrassment. They need also to know that the parents are there to support and help them out instead of giving punishments. It should never be underestimate the role of children's friends that sometime can help revealing more detail about the social life of children.

4.1.4 Online video games

Online video games, as the ordinary video games, can generate addiction and can alter the personality, in particular for teens and pre-teens. Indeed, a shy child can became extrovert and passive child can became violent.

In brief, online games generate two major problems when players do not use the right behavior and families do not properly educate children.

The first problem is **addiction** and this can generate situation of: mood swing, social isolation, compulsive game playing and diminished imagination. Some doctors define excess gaming when the time dedicated to this activity is above one hour per day.

The second potential problem is the risk to become victim of **phishing or stealing** in general. For example, in 2011 Play Station network was attacked by hackers to steal personal information from 77 m accounts and the service network was temporary shut down for 24 days.

There is also the risk to install malware on personal devices while they download applications and protect from this it is important to read the users' feedback, check the reputation of the software developer and, in case of mobile devices, download applications from store associated to the operative system.

4.1.5 Online Predators

According to Dr. Michael C. Seto, almost the 1% of world male population has pedophilic temptation and considering that the world male population is 3.5 billion the 1% represents 35 million people. These people express their desire also through web communities, which they share same interests and where they can exchange images, techniques, fantasies and also children. These communities exist and act in the anonymity of the Internet and SM are used to create opportunities for approaching and stay in contact with victims. Minors are at risk because their capability to use SM, the lack of parental control and the poor experience to handle difficult situations. The predators feel safe with SM because the approach and the relationship established with the victim are anonymous and there is nothing in common with the exposure on the streets. The use of a fake I.D. does not preclude anyone meeting anybody else using SNs. Actually, SNs make possible to share what the user is doing and what is the current location.

According to Crimes Against Children Research Center (Mitchell, Jones, Finkelhor, & Wolak, 2014) one in eleven young Internet users (9% of the total respondents) received an unwanted sexual solicitation in 2010 and the 3% received aggressive sexual solicitations only in UK.

In summary, regarding this section there are two considerations to make:

1. The unrestricted number of personal contacts can favor new ideas, business, and motivations but also can develop treats and inconvenience for users because it is possible that strangers are added to personal networks but they do not have good intentions.
2. The appropriate parental control and the understanding of the importance of personal privacy are fundamental, in particular for teenagers and pre-teen, to protect them from online predators.

4.1.6 Disturbing Content

SM content is populated with different materials by the actions of many different people. This means that it is possible to bump into disturbing image and video, where cruel, violent and sexist are the most common.

This content could cause anxiety and worry in the viewer, in particular for young people because most of the time they are not able to contextualise the online message. In particular, children can develop aggressiveness or fearfulness.

Besides the well-known attention to TV's content it is also a good practice if parents can monitor their children's activities on the Internet and talk to them about the scenes and content when it is appropriate. It is extremely important educate children to use the Internet and social media rather than rely on the Internet's blocks and filters.

4.1.7 Phishing and Fraud

Criminals have opportunities to use SM for gaining information on victims because SNs show personal detail and information that can be sufficient for stealing personal identity or know the right time for sneaking in the victim's house.

For example, Facebook reveal information such as: name, surname, current city, date of birth, marital status, current geographic location, employer, siblings' names, personal telephone number and email address. LinkedIn has other public information, such as: personal connections and updated career path.

Phishing is a criminal method for obtaining personal and financial information and it is described as any act for attempt to steal personal information through the web with the purpose of identity theft and to gain access of banking account.

Criminals use fake emails or fake web sites to steal information from unaware users while they are typing personal and financial information.

To protect from these scams it is recommended using common sense and first of all, never reveal bank account's detail and PIN and when consumers use web sites they need to verify that there is *"https://"* at the beginning of the web address or the padlock in the browser window. Furthermore, they need to verify if the web address is genuine, this means it does not contain extra-words or a strange combination of numbers and letters. Another good recommendation is to avoid opening, or clicking, of unusual messages that can be present in the own inbox.

RFID identity theft (wireless identity theft) is a system for stealing information regarding credit card and debit card, which have a wireless feature. This technology uses electronic recording systems (available also for smartphones) that capture information when they are at close range from the cards even if they are in purses or wallets. This wireless system is able to get data, such as: the name present on card, expiration date and security code and all these data are used to clone a new card or to purchase online.

This new stealing method began when the major credit card companies adopted the contactless payment system to speed up payments' transactions. Indeed, RFID uses radio frequency for transmitting the account's information, located in a chip, up to the machine "Point Of Sale".

Not many consumers know that smart phones are enabled to the technology **NFC** (compatible with RFID protocol) for transmitting and receiving small amounts of data between two devices. This data transmission works only if the devices are within few centimeters from each other and there is no need of pair code to establish the communication like Bluetooth requires.

In particular, for payments transmission (i.e. processing and receiving normal payments) this technology needs dedicated payment applications, for example MasterCard *"Paypass"*.

On the other end, this technology offers advantages to digital pickpockets because they only need to modify the phone's firmware and install an open source application (easy to find on the Internet) for reading credit and debit card data, present in the microchip.

In general, the NFC system is made available to make the payments easier for users but it creates also a data security dilemma.

4.1.8 Other Inconveniences

When people do not realise the power of SM, some pleasant events can turn into nightmares and can have nasty conclusions.

For example, in Hamburg (Germany) a sixteen years old girl used FB to send a public invitation for her house party with full address attached. The night before the event, almost 15.000 people accepted the invitation.

On the day of the event, even if it was cancelled, one thousand people showed up to her doorstep from the 7p.m. until 2a.m. for joining the party. The massive presence of people on the street generated consequences, indeed many properties were damaged and fights took place. A video, of this massive crowd is still present online (Al Jazeera English, 2011).

Another similar example happened in 2008, when a birthday party, of a girl 16 years old, was advertised on Facebook. The situation took a turn for the worse when four hundreds uninvited attendee joined his party.

The Daily Mail gave prominence to the event (Millis, 2008) and reported that the house of the birthday girl was heavily damaged and it took 12 police cars to calm down the situation.

The article informed also that there are groups of guys looking for this kind of events to sneak in the houses and create damages.

4.2 How to protect from Social Media's threats

SM are new channels of communication that join the information media group and criminals may use them to steal personal information because they are two way communication channels. To protect ourselves from these possible attacks we need to use common sense, for example not revealing bank account's details and PIN and when accessing web sites make sure the presence of *"https://"* at the beginning of the web address or the padlock in the browser window. Moreover, check if the web address is genuine and it has not extra words or a strange combination of numbers and letters. Not open, or click, unusual message that you find in your inbox although human curiosity can push to do it.

Furthermore, there are also other threats to consider and to pay extra attention even if they can appear boring or over-protective. A summary is reported below:

1. Consider the right level of information privacy during an interaction and use SNs settings to change your preferences accordingly. Avoid that personal data are advertised publically, which can make you an easy target for criminals who want steal identity or objects.

2. Evaluate the advertisement of pictures and comments because, as said in the past chapters, what is online stays online.

3. Keep a good online reputation because this is part of the life. This means that your business, activity, reputation can be affected by comments present on the Internet and on SM in particular.

4. Take action in case of harassment. Delete the contact from your list and block it. Report the case to the site manager.

5. Dose the use of SM to avoid an over usage of them and then prevent from addiction.

6. Do not underestimate the importance of the face to face communication and respect the interlocutor avoiding stay involved in SM conversation during the discussion.

7. Protect the device you are using with passwords and encryptions in order to protect sensitive data in case of loss of the device.

8. Always use the common sense during the interactions to avoid awkward situation or make feel uncomfortable the counterpart.

4.3 Social Media and Data Privacy

Protection of data privacy and social media do not get along and do not share the same scopes for obvious reasons. People use SNs because they choose to be visible for other users and available for communication. For these scopes, users must enrich SNs profiles with personal information and this generates a data base. Sometimes users can decide the level of information to provide but because the SM success and the growing interest around these new media, the protection of the personal information is becoming less important for some people. Indeed, according to Pew Research Center (Madden, et al., 2013), on 802 US teens aged between 12-17 years old, the research revealed that this category tends to share publicly more personal information than the others. The research highlights also that the number of personal information, publically shared by this group of teens, is also higher than before the arrival of social media. In particular, the main findings are:

- The 40% of teens have a public profile on FB.
- Only 9% of the panel is very concern about personal data viewed by third parties.
- The 91% of users share pictures of themselves (in 2006 this number was 79%).
- The 71% post their school name (up from 49% in 2006.

- The 71% post the city or town where they live (up from 61% in 2006).
- The 53% post their email address (up from 29% in 2006).
- The 20% post their mobile phone number (up from 2% in 2006).
- The 92% post their real name on the SNs they use most.
- The 84% post their interests, such as: movies, music, or favorite books.
- The 82% post their birth date.
- The 62% post their relationship status.
- The 24% post videos of themselves.
- Teens (aged between 14-17 years old) post more personal information than the younger ones (aged 12 and 13 years old), in particular:

    o The16% of teens provides their current location in the post.

Fig. 17 shows a graphical comparison between the year 2012 and 2006 for content posted by teens on their Social Networks pages.

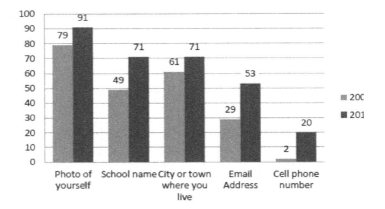

Source: Madden, et al., 2013

Figure 16 – Contents posted by Teens on SN

Apart the quantity and the quality of personal information revealed by users, there is also a security aspect to consider regarding the personal data publically available. There are situation when information are collected and analysed for gaining an unfair advantage by third parties or situation where, even if the cause is noble or for public utility (like preventing or fight criminality), can generate abuse and excess if not regulated appropriately.

Recently I attended a group discussion regarding the topic *"SM and information privacy"* and I learned that some of the participants were favorable to give away their data privacy completely if this improves the crime prevention. For example, they were favorable of having their personal conversations monitored by national agencies or third parties and be located through a GPS tracker system present in mobile phones or under the skin if this helps with security. According to them, because they are honest and good citizens, they are not worried to be watched or monitored constantly. While they were talking, I noticed an angry expression on their faces as they suffered a recent violence or criminal event. I was interested in that conversation and I wanted to understand more about their thoughts and I asked to them if they had been victim of criminal episode recently and the answer was negative. Then, I asked the reason they need all those precautions and, at unanimity, they told me they heard bad stories on the radio and TV; their beliefs were based on statistics, of which they knew a little.

I realised that they certainties were generated by the emotion and it was almost impossible to discuss further with them because the idea was made. For my interlocutors the technology is the answer to any threats, despite the level of risk or the origin of the threat. For them, it is not important to know who monitors their communication (e.g. government agency or private company) and how their recordings are managed and where they are stored.

For example, only twenty years ago few categories of people had to record their fingerprints. Among them there were criminals and soldiers because they have committed a crime or because they could have been recognised in case of death on duty. The good and honest citizens were preserved from registration because there were not reasons to include them also. Today this, and other data, must be provided by almost every adult, for example, to access in some countries or for just a layover.

What would happen to our democracy if the organizations responsible for collection and analysis of data did not do a proper job? Holding sensitive information means also have more power than others. This is one of the main reasons why it is important a clear regulation that disciplines the use of information, which categories of people can be monitored and what information it is possible to collect.

Besides this, there is also the case that criminals can breach into private communications and, combined with information available online, can steal I.D., blackmailing the victim, coercing someone to commit specific actions, manipulating newspapers and personal opinions, stealing industrial secrets, etc.

Furthermore, give away too many personal details can give companies the possibility of using them for data mining and profiling. This is not the case of understand the consumer needs but taking unfair advantage of others because the two parties do not share the same information access and typology. The business relationship, for example, can be affected by this deep knowledge of information and actions could be taken in advance based on: medical condition, location, marital status, addictions, ethnic group, religion, financial status, education, political view and behavior. In this way, companies can maximize their profit because they can target better consumers for marketing campaign or adjusting constantly the price of goods and services based on users' preference and Internet activities.

In the 95% of conversations, people say nothing confidential or to be ashamed of but even though, an individual has the right to know if someone else is on the communication.

In order to protect sensitive personal information from criminals or from companies' tracking systems, there are some methods available, such as:

1. Use encrypted emails and anonymous web sites for chatting;
2. Use trusted search engines that do not share information with third parties (E.g. DuckDuckGo, Ixquick, Startpage, Tor Browser or the European email service Bitmessage or Riseup). Usually, common search engines store the Internet IP address, which identifies the device's location, the number of activities done and the typology.
3. Be aware that mobile phone and a SIM card can profile users. The first one has a unique number (IMEI), which can track the user and the SIM card store information about the mobile service subscriber. When the mobile device accesses the network it also transmits information to the network provider, such as: browsing, texting, calls and connection time.
4. Install apps from recognized apps stores and read the permission request of such apps. They can ask for more permission than what they need to run.

In summary, there are four different security typologies to consider:

1. **Behavioral**, keep the use of connected devices at minimum;

2. **Technological Equipment**, make sure that the devices are not physically tampered;

3. **Data Transmission**, use encryptions.

4. **Network**, avoid or block applications that store and track the navigation history or that transmit

information automatically. Watch out for the free applications because they could include malware.

It is important to understand that unregulated mass acquisition of sensitive personal data marks a violation of data privacy and also can cause damages and destabilization for the:

1. **International economy system**. In wrong hands, the data can favor few companies or people and they can affect the free market and the quality of the services. Few subjects would be rewarded based on illicit rather than merit.
2. **Foreign Diplomacy**. Foreign negotiations and agreements would be reached with an unnatural method. On long term, this does not only twist the win-win negotiation but it can generate a diplomatic conflict between countries and organisations.
3. **Society**. The excess and unregulated monitoring could undermine the democracy. Powerful men, could have the temptation to use this information to limit the population's freedom for a personal profit or advantages.

4.3.1 Surveillance programs

In an interview with TV Network *RT*, Julian Assange defined FB as: "*the most appalling spy machine that has ever been invented*" (RT, 2011). He considers FB a powerful database where people are happy to store their personal data.

In September 2014, a report of United Nation (Emmerson, 2014) revealed that mass surveillance programs do not respect the right of the online privacy. A month later, Ben Emmerson (Special Rapporteur on the promotion and protection of Human Right while countering terrorism) during the presentation of his report to the General Assembly body, dealing with cultural, social and humanitarian issues, stated: *"Measures that interfere with the right to privacy must be authorized by accessible and precise domestic law that pursues a legitimate aim, is proportionate and necessary"* (UN News Centre, 2014). According to this report, Emmerson believes that the mass surveillance programs can be justified in principle for fighting international terrorism but they also erode the right to the privacy.

Furthermore, he maintains that the Member States have the obbligation to provide detailed justifications and evidences to have their citizens under surveillance and he also suggests to create an independent oversight body with the responsibility to review these justifications before their applications.

In 2013, the former NSA computer specialist Edward Snowden made public the biggest secret of world surveillance system, which the main scope is to capture and record social media data of the entire world population.

This section is not about the reason of this revelation but analyses the impact of this surveillance systems for the society.

The surveillance systems were developed for monitoring people and it does not matter if someone has been a good person and never been convicted. Despite all that, apparently there are unknown subjects, which are free to decide who must be spied and for how long. Apparently also the politicians knew a little about these programs; indeed when the scandal raised also the US President Obama appeared unprepared and uncomfortable talking about these programs.

The main threat for the people is not if those systems work for Countries' military ambitions, but that those systems target everyone, despite people innocence, the age and other characteristics. In summary, those systems violate one of the most important and fundamental societal achievements, which is the **right for the data privacy**.

In theory, the surveillance programs were developed to fulfill the needs of homeland security of UK and US and to fight against world terrorism. In practice, based on the amount and typology of information recorded and the category of people spied these programs suggest different scopes. Indeed, Prime Ministers of ally coalition, big corporations and diplomatic organisations were also among the targets of these systems.

On 25th of October 2013, the newspaper "Il Mattino" published an article of the former president of EU commission Romano Prodi, who maintains that those surveillance systems work against the international law and against the fundamental rights of the people. In his article, Prodi reveals a personal anecdote to prove that those systems were created and implemented not only to fight terrorism but also for acquiring confidential information regarding business and diplomacy.

Prodi, reveals that when he was in Jerusalem, for an official visit, he received a call from Gian Maria Gros-Pietro (chairman of the Italian oil giant ENI) for a confidential discussion on ongoing company business. The company was in competition with a big American oil company for a business deal, which included the oil extraction and processing for one of the major oil producing country in the world. Gro-Pietro called Prodi for asking his intervention to close the business deal but this was not necessary because ENI won the deal few days later. Weeks later, a weekly magazine revealed the entire discussion that Prodi had on the phone with Gros-Pietro. The article was very accurate and Prodi asked to a qualified telecom engineer, who worked for the European Commission, how it was possible to have the entire conversation recorded and the answer was that his voice had to be set for recording during the use of digital communication systems.

On the other side of the Atlantic, also the representative of ENI in US was called by his American competitor to demand the reason the company asked the intervention of the President of European Commission.

According to the former CIA and NSA computer specialist Snowden, the illegal surveillance is conduct using some of the most powerful programs owned by USA government. I summarise the most important ones below:

- o **PRISM**. This program collects the Internet contents, which are stored in companies' database and provides also an analysis of such contents. To be effective, it needs the data of the major tech companies, which support the information's sharing between users. According to *The Guardian* (Rusche, 2013), the access was granted by big IT corporations like Google, YouTube (Google), Facebook, Microsoft, PalTalk, AOL, Skype (Microsoft), Apple and Yahoo. These companies declared they were unaware about the purposes of these data acquisitions from government organizations. After these revelations, some companies announced that they will not grant anymore a direct access to their information.
- o **XKeyscore**. This program is capable of monitoring any user and any activity on the Internet in real time (The Guardian, 2013). To be specific, the system searches and stores data, such as: e-mails content and activities on the Internet. Furthermore, it is able to search for metadata in the Internet and during phone communication (i.e. time, sender and recipient). The program runs on a Linux cluster and there are 500 of

them distributed around the world. Due to the increase of information generated on the Internet, the system is scalable. Compared to the other systems, the key feature of this program is that it is highly accurate during the analyses of contents. The program targets users that utilise, for example, any form of data encryption, use a language different from the one typically spoken in his location and who search suspicious subjects on the Internet. The information is stored from 3 to 5 days and the metadata for 30 days. In case of interesting material, this can be retained in others database for almost five years.

In his first interview to The Guardian (Greenwald, 2013), Snowden said: *"I, sitting at my desk, could wiretap anyone, from you or your accountant, to a federal judge or even the President, if I had a personal email"*. This statement gives an idea about the low level of security of personal information and the high level of discretion that a specialist has in the name of national security.

- **Tempora.** It is a project with the goal to capture large amounts of data in particular from web and phone. According to the The Guardian (MacAskill, Borger, Hopkins, Davies, & Ball, 2013), this system has been used by the British intelligence agency *"Government Communication Headquarter"* (GCHQ) and the American partner NSA. This system is able to filter the content of fiber-optic cables transmission. It can analyse and store content for up 30 days. Also Tempora was developed to monitor anyone despite to be a suspect or not.

In addition to the three systems described above, which have the scope of information gathering, there are also programs developed specifically for information analysis. Among them, the two most used are:

- **Boundless Informant.** It is a software and according to Greenwald and MacAskill (2013) this examines data collected by Electronic Surveillance Program (this data is called DNI) and the information gathered by telephone calls (this data is called DNR). The two authors inform also that in March 2013, the NSA collected a total DNI of 97.11 b and 124.8 b of DNR. Fig. 18 shows the level of surveillance for the Countries under monitoring and the color goes from green (least coverage) to red (most intensive).

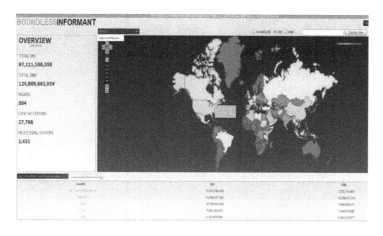

Source: Greenwald & MacAskill, 2013

Figure 17 – "Boundless Informant" application

- **Biometric Recognition Systems.** They are used for data scanning of SM in order to identify criminal or national security threats. For this scope, they process biological and behavioral traits, for example voice, face, iris, and fingerprints. The way they work is very intuitive because the data acquired is compared with a reference database to find possible matching. The systems are based on probability, this mean that the results could have margins of error.

Besides the ethic doubts, there are also some legal concerns how these systems operate because, by US law, any US citizen cannot be subject of surveillance without a warrant and the use made of those systems is not comply with this regulation.

Moreover, because the use of surveillance programs is not regulated by the ordinary law, there is a potential risk to use them to limit human rights or to force actions and decisions among the population. In this contest, there is the risk that unknown people could decide, for example, to have under surveillance all the contacts of a suspect even without evidences of involvement.

The majority of world population could believe these programs do not concern them as long as they are not criminals, but they have also to consider that people have to live in a society of law. The history is full of examples of populations that have fought for their freedom and for safeguard of human rights and one of the main roles of a democratic Country is to guarantee these societal achievements. Surveillance is one of methods to prevent crime or to catch criminals but it must be also regulated by low to avoid excess.

Chapter Five

Are Social Media Temporary Phenomena?

Social Media are the target of critics today who believe that they are unnecessary for societal change and that they do not bring any real or tangible benefit, and from others who really believe in them because are part of technology and of social revolution.

The fact is that they are part of media in general and have specific characteristics, which were described in chapter 2. They are young trend and are under study and development to explore their limits and applications. New research and investment has made it possible to associate SM to artificial intelligence, in the sense that they support communication between smart devices supporting these to take decisions on the base of specific input received. This chapter analyses all of the above aspects and give ideas for possible future scenarios.

5.1 Critics

SM are an extraordinary collection of innovative communication tools and in my opinion (as I will show in the next section) they still have room for improvement because their application can be extended also to objects and not only humans.

In contrast, there are people who are very critical about SM because they maintain SM do not improve society.

Some of the worst critiques come from two different categories of people:

a) People close to traditional media corporations, who are not fully objective because they are in conflict with the new media;

b) The older generation that, in some cases, finds it hard to even turn on a desktop.

One of my favourite writers, Malcom Gladwell, wrote an article in The New Yorker regarding his thoughts about SM (Gladwell, 2010). I want to recall a few key points of this article that have impressed me. In particular, the author supports the idea that SM are not important for society to change, and he uses historic cases to demonstrate this theory. He maintains that the many cases of activisms, or civil-rights, movements were successful without the use of SM. However, I must say that the events described in the article, happened when SM were not even developed or conceived of.

For example, during the civil-right movement and environmental movement of 1960s, only traditional media, like local TV, radio and newspapers, existed to spread opinions and make people aware of events. What I am saying is that any human era has its form of media and others will be developed based on the technology available at the time. For the complexity, the size and the organisation of today's society, traditional media is probably not sufficient for communication. Today, SM can trigger revolutions, punish police brutality (caught on video), and support a candidate's election campaign.

SM are part of media's group and their scope set by the users to use it for good or bad goals.

Gladwell also wrote: "*social media are not about this kind of hierarchical organization* [e.g. civil-right movements]. *Facebook and the like are tools for building networks, which are the opposite, in structure and character, of hierarchies. Unlike hierarchies, with their rules and procedures, networks aren't controlled by a single central authority. Decisions are made through consensus, and the ties that bind people to the group are loose*".

In the author's view, an achievement is possible only if there is a leader that coordinates the public demand and support. He points to the absence of hierarchy in social media system with a central authority able to think strategically.

To give an idea, the author believes that social media are able to provide pieces of a puzzle and there is nobody able to put all together in order to get the final picture.

In my opinion, the power of SM is regarding its scope and utility more than, for example, the quality of relationships between contacts. To say this in another way: **the aim of SM is to establish collaborative connections in order to benefit from them**. Furthermore, SM is a group of media, and therefore they must be evaluated as such. This means the evaluation must be done through a comparison with other media.

The logic behind SM is to be an alternative to hierarchies' approach and to guarantee that every member of the social network is the leader. Contrary to the hierarchical approach, SM favour democracy and every user can express opinion and the decisions are taken on majority bases. For example, the groups are created for common needs, common goals or social movement (e.g. anti-globalisation, anti-water privatisation, anti-Genetically Modified Organism) and their strategy is agreed by members.

SM are applications that facilitate the communication, for example they can record conversations, make documents sharable, comment life events and group's decisions. Sometimes a group spokesman is necessary but this is agreed and voted by the members. Contrary to the hierarchical organization, SM favour a bottom-up approach.

Looking back at media's history, there is a close relationship with technology; specifically, a medium maintains its popularity until a new and more effective technology is developed.

Moreover, people tend to use the most appropriate medium which they believe will get the information they need and in the time they want. This means that nowadays, SM represent the most advanced source of information, as they can provide information quickly and accurately.

5.2   SM and Artificial Intelligence

SM were created with the purpose of connecting people but, with recent developments of technology and software applications, it is possible also the interaction with smart devices and establish a communication between them. This is a new frontier for our society because this transforms a consolidated interaction system into a wider concept beyond our imagination. This scenario represents the next level for SM and it improves artificial intelligence (AI). This because we have made it possible for one or more smart devices to: communicate, exchange information with other smart devices (creating, in this way, a community of devices), making decisions and predict events.

Under a different perspective, SNs capture a significant quantity of users' information but this data is not structured and this means it is very difficult to put to use. Because of this issue, companies use **Artificial Intelligent** (A.I.) techniques to analyse SNs. These have extraordinary learning capacities, indeed these techniques are capable to process all the activities occurring over their networks and they are capable to analyse conversations, process facial recognition, and analyse gaming activity. In general, according to Schalkoff (1990) the scope of A.I. study is to *"explain and emulate intelligent behavior in terms of computational processes"* through performing the tasks of decision making, problem solving and learning. When applied to SNs, A.I. uses social computing and data mining techniques for the analysis. The outcomes support marketer studies to identify influential profiles, within networks, and use appropriate societal marketing approach to reach these individuals. The applications used by A.I. to study users' behaviors foster the discussion of ethics, in particular for the threat to **privacy** and threat to **human dignity.** Indeed, any single users' activity (even if the user is anonymous) increases the quantity of information available for a data mining analysis and improves the accuracy of predictions for single user. There is also the high risk that I.A. can replace humans' presence in significant jobs (e.g. police officer, judge and soldier) because its capability to analyse fast and well the people's behaviors, and this would create frustration and alienation in the society. A.I. is impersonal and this means that it is limited to analyse and to act according to the programming. Indeed, machines associate a specific action to a specific event.

SN companies are investing in AI to make their applications more advanced and to benefit from a unique selling proposition.

For example, Facebook launched a new research lab for this purpose, and appointed as head of this lab Yann LeCun, who is a computer scientist and a former full-time professor at New York University.

Google acquired DeepMind for $400m and, with this acquisition, it has secured control of a company with the biggest concentration of researchers, who work on projects for recognising faces in videos and words in human speech. The ambitious goal of DeepMind is to find the ways to develop real AI. For this, research has to develop a machine which is able to understand human language and make decisions on its own. The company wants to capture and reproduce the activities of neurons present in the neocortex, where 80% of the brain's thinking happens. The combination of the existing group of highly skilled scientists working on AI and the possibility of additional resources, which Google can guarantee to the project, makes the research promising.

In 2014 LinkedIn purchased for $120m the startup company Bright.com, which is aligned to LinkedIn's strategy to expand the network of professional content and also its product range. In particular, Bright.com specialises in developing data and algorithms to improve job match searching. This startup is different because its solution uses a special method to find a better match between candidates and jobs using a combination of data science and machine learning algorithms.

Another SM company, Pinterest, has decided to invest in AI by purchasing VisualGraph, a company that specialises in visual search and image recognition. Pinterest commented that this acquisition was made to better understand what users "pin" in order to show customised ads and to suggest appropriate content.

Nowadays, there are many smart devices that collect information from people and transmit it to other smart devices to build a database and produce statistics. The new implementations and the new devices developed are for: well-being, transportation, entertainments, houses and work.

In particular:

a) **Well-Being**. There are devices that are able to collect and transmit personal physical information. For example, company Withings has developed devices which track sleep to monitor and improve sleep quality. These devices are based on the connection and interaction between sleep sensor, bedside device and smartphone application. The combination of lighting and sound, generated by the bedside device, induces sleep and provides a stress-free wake up. A sensor under the bed monitors the sleep cycle through body movement, breathing and heartrate analysis; the bedside devices analyses the temperature, sounds and the light level through the night to better understand what makes for a better sleep. The results are showed on the user's smartphone.

Another example is a body analyser which can calculate the user's weight, body fat, and heartrate, and air quality in the room, and store the data to show on a smart phone.

Another company, Fitbit, also provides smart devices for fitness, which provide GPS tracking and monitors heartrate. They also track all the day's activities, monitor sleep automatically and provide statistics to better manage daily life. For the same area, the world leader in consumer technology and wearable devices, Jambone, has developed "Up", which is a flexible rubber-coated wristband that collects data such as: sleeping, eating and daily activity and sends it to software applications for the iPhone and Android devices to calculate and present results.

b) **Transportation.** The development of new technologies for the transportation system and the progress made by social media applications are the two main contributors for a radical change of the private transport.

Among the companies, the race to offer driverless cars to the market is just started and Apple, Google, Tesla and Uber are some of main companies involved in this challenge.

The above companies need partners in automakers to progress further because they do not have skills for the production of these. For the first time since the creation of the automobile, people has to rethink the purpose and usage of this vehicle. Indeed, most of the past transport developments were based on mechanic and environmental implementations (e.g. construction of railroads, electric lights implementation, and improvement of engines performance and vehicle's comfort for the passengers) but it was not conceived to give free time to the driver, this means offering him/her free time for reading books, watching video, catnap, writing, etc.

Besides the additional time for leisure, companies want also reduce the risk of accidents because the vehicle's movement is coordinated with the ones around and because it can move also if the visual condition is not perfect (e.g. fog, night and rain).

Because the communication with other vehicles, the car can reduce the time travel and the search of an available parking spot. Additional drones can move loads around the country and decreasing the number of vehicles on the road.

Among the IT companies, Google is the one in better condition to provide in short time self-driving cars to the market because the company has mapping databases, artificial intelligence know-how, and its fleet of driverless cars.

This is also the time to decide which kind of vehicles produce and at moment there are two approaches:

1. The first one, gradual semi-autonomous, it is supported by car developers (and by Tesla in particular) believes that driver-assisting technologies (advanced cruise control and functionalities like the Mercedes-Benz S-Class *"traffic jam assist"*) should be added to existent

vehicles and a pure driverless system should be reached only over time.

2. The second approach, ground-up (led by Google) believes that a complete new car needs to be produced because there are so many technology developments available that does not make sense use the same concept of vehicle. Indeed, new features involve all the aspect of the car, for example breaks, ignition, steering wheels and tires.

At this point would be interesting understand if people would feel comfortable travelling in a driverless vehicle and if this technology is 100% reliable today. When Google tested this technology, the company made sign to the passengers a contract and this stated clearly that people in the car must be alert while the driverless system was on because it that was an experiment and in an early stage of implementation. If something goes wrong drivers must take the control of the vehicles (would you go on a pilot free airplane, for example?).

Apparently the idea that passengers can enjoy free time on board of the vehicle collide with the reality that someone has to be ready to take control of the vehicle in case of necessity and this grey area is simple unacceptable for personal safety.

As for many new technologies at early stage, even if these are available on the market does not necessary mean that people is ready for them or satisfy current needs.

It is really hard to predict when this kind of vehicles will be ready for the consumers, even if some companies are really confident that in 5 years the first cars will be available in showrooms.

There are also other examples of SM application to transportation system. For example, Boeing (using the "Phantom Works" division) is developing prototypes of vehicles that are able to fly and drive on the road. Vehicles are capable of exchanging information, such as GPS location, and following a programmed route to avoid possible impacts.

Nissan's CARWINGS®, for electric cars, is a service that enables a smartphone to act as a remote control and use functions like: checking the status of the battery, starting the fan for the climate control or checking the charging level. Apple has developed a specific system that links the car with an iPhone in order to communicate through the car itself. The system uses voice control, touch screen, knobs, dials or buttons. The connection with the smartphone will allow the use of Apple maps, calling, reading and writing messages (with listening and writing modes) playing music and other supported apps.

c) **Smart House**. For this category, the implementation of SM is advanced. Indeed, a centralised software system has already been developed that is capable of handling some of the needs of those who live in the house. The developer is Brian Conte (CEO of Fast Track) and the system is called Cleopatra, and this interacts with people through an avatar present on TV, tablet or computer screen. The system acquires information automatically via motion sensors and microphones in the house and through special bracelets worn by members of the family. Specifically, it informs about incoming calls, plays music by voice commands, sets timers for lights and turns on appliances. It knows who is in the house and recognises visitors at the front door.

While Cleopatra is only one computer, Microsoft is developing the idea of including in the home more "smart devices". These, for example, cover entire walls in bedrooms, illuminating the room with colour to match any mood and occasion, or to show favourite pictures. They also recognise when someone is about to cook and will provide help (for example, they automatically project the recipes onto the counter, reading them out and turning on the oven).

As shown in the innovation centre in a demonstration called "livingtomorrow", the house will come to life because it will be built with smart devices, such as bathrooms with mirrors that show the news and temperature and refrigerators that can read food labels and give product information (price, the nearest shop where the product is available and the expiration date) thanks to RFID. Purchases are made electronically by writing what it is needed and this message will be sent to the supermarket that will deliver the shopping directly to the home.

A smart house contains smart devices, which are connected to each other through the exchange of information. On the way home, for example, it could activate the microwave to heat a dish, or activate the iron automatically when the dryer stops.

d) **Work**. Work also will change, as it will be possible to make greater use of telepresence and holograms which will reduce the need to travel. In fact, a doctor will be able to operate surgically using robotics and telepresence.

e) **Entertainment**. The entertainment industry, together with the military and medical industry, is investing in development of devices which are able to improve the virtual reality through sensation and stimulus.
These new communication devices, for example, transmit through a smart oar the feeling of rowing on a river, or special jackets, with a built-in airbag, can transmit the sensation of being in combat because these inflate or deflate at specific points of the body to recreate the sensation of touch.

The research and innovation do not stop there; there has been development of a new form of communication through thought. This is the case of the Australian company Emotiv Systems, which has developed a "brain-computer interface" based on electro-encephalography. The product is similar to a helmet with 16 electrodes attached, and acts as input for a computer. Because every emotion or sensation felt by the user is an electrical signal developed by the brain, this is recognized and captured by helmet, which transmits it to a computer and then translates it into commands. This means that the management of a computer or sending data to other users can be done through the directions that come with the thought.

There is a new development for those who want to take the best pictures and videos, because these can be done using a drone. This is a new trend and the software platform *"Dronestagram"* is dedicated to the collection and sharing of this material. This new trend has the scope to show the world from another perspective.

f) **More Hardware Platforms for SM connection.** Google is developing a new era of glasses (Google Glass) with the possibility of using all the Google functionality, such as maps, emails and Internet access. The purpose is to have a hands-free, mobile device for daily activities. At the time of writing, the project is still in progress, and this means that the final goal is not yet clear. Apparently, the glasses have no GPS chip but will contain Bluetooth and Wi-Fi. Google stated that there will be not be any feature to take pictures or for facial recognition. It is not hard to imagine a future device with its own SIM card and, when we meet somebody, we can have their personal file taken from some SN or private database projected on the lens, just as anticipated by the movie Terminator (see Fig. 19).

Source: Cameron (1984)

Figure 18 - Frame taken from the movie Terminator

This invention could trigger a new era of mobile devices because other companies can start from this and develop a more appealing product and enrich the smart devices with more features.

For example, using a smart phone to recognise a street and, combined with SN data, knowing who lives there (see Fig.20).

Figure 19 - Future Scenario for a Social Network

Nowadays, the trend is that of integrating devices with an Internet connection, and this has the effect of boosting SM usage even more. For example the system **"In car Internet services"**, developed by Cadillac (Cadillac Wi-Fi) and Chrysler (Chrysler Uconnect Web), are able to provide Wi-Fi access to people in and around the car so that the passenger can send emails, browse the Internet and watch a video.

They have huge potential to replace or be competitor of navigator systems or to be used to send accurate car location data in the case of a breakdown.

However, the market also offers mobile hotspots that could be installed on the main motorways to give Wi-Fi to the passengers and car.

As seen in the previous examples, objects are fully involved in SM transformation, because they are "terminal users" or vehicles for SM communication. Also, these new "users" respect the same rules:

1. They transmit and receive data;
2. They need software applications as an interface and data elaboration;
3. They are always available and the communication is quick,
4. They still need the Internet to work.

5.3 Benefit for the Community

To be a real benefit for the people, SM have to satisfy people's needs or be an effective vehicle to satisfy those needs. Studies in the 1900s developed the concept of "goal orientation". According to Atkinson (1964), the motivational trigger for people is to achieve their goals. People behave for a specific purpose in order to reach a level of satisfaction, and this purpose should be obvious, otherwise the behaviour itself will stop. This means that people continue to use SM to achieve their goal (e.g. friendship, business and entertainment) and the moment SM become useless to achieve the goal people desist using them.

A part this theory, to explain the success and the potential benefit for the community, is the **emotional component**. In fact, the use of SM, and in particular SNs, can be seen as the alleviation of pain (the reward-punishment system). This means that a perception of emotional lack is filled by connecting to friends and family though SM. The same process starts when a person is, for example, thirsty or hungry.

To use a theory from Aristotle, the emotional effect is also explained with the "movement". This means that people act to satisfy pleasure and to remove the things which produce pain. Based on this theory, I believe that people use SM because they do not produce pain, otherwise they would stop using them.

Among SNs users, there is a part that really enjoys these network platforms because they feel closer to friends and family. This was impossible to believe a few years ago. Sharing personal lives help to build stronger relationships with others.

Besides all of this, there are physical and mental limitations to using SM and, in particular, SNs. Indeed, remaining always connected with others, replying to their comments and sending messages takes time. Furthermore, excess SM usage can create boredom or detract time from fulfilling other needs, pursuing other interests, or just relaxing by, for example, reading a nice book.

Keeping track of or interacting with hundreds of personal connections is physically impossible. For this reason, people started to apply the method used in real life to the virtual life; in fact, they limit interactions only to the ones they feel very close to and for whom they can dedicate more time.

Nowadays, SM are quite indispensable for business and society because these are globalised. This means that as people are interconnected globally. Despite of that, SM are still a media, this means that people should use them when needed and turn them off afterwards.

Chapter Six

Conclusion

As mentioned in the introduction, this book wanted to give the reader a new prospective of SM through different points of view and showing different SM applications.

There are a combination of communities and networks that support the sharing and spreading of information between people and smart devices (even if it will take more time for a complete and extended application to these objects). Too often SM are confused with SNs or they are limited by the definition of SN but as stated in Chapter One, they are something more extensive. Indeed, they do not represent a sum of single communities but they also represent a vehicle that gives to everyone (for those with the Internet connection at least) the possibility to acquire information and interact with someone outside of their trusted circle.

Despite the previous attempt to build forms of SM, today they have found the right combination of elements that has made their success possible, and these key elements are: the current technology that made smart devices possible; the increase of the Internet penetration in the population; the increase in world youth population; an economy based on globalisation; and the enlightenment of the current society that demands freedom, independency and application of human rights.

An excursus on the evolution of communication models has revealed how SM were adapted to them and the main changes they made. In particular, SM reduce the time from "sender" to "receiver", and they guarantee reciprocity in communication because the receiver can also become the sender, and so on. Another aspect to consider is that there is no limit to the distance between the sender and the receiver. Is also important to keep in mind that SM are oriented to people that use devices with the Internet connection and this could be a limitation for people, but they also offer an element for better targeting.

The reasons that push people to communicate (and use SM) are found in four practical situations:

1. **Physical need.** People try to stay in contact with people that make feel them better due to the positive communication they have, and this influences them to improve their mood, reduce the stress, or receive the right dose of motivation for the day.

2. **Identity need.** This means that people seek a confrontation with others regarding, for example, career success, life experience and how resolve common problems. This need is triggered by a sense of "check-up", in that they want to comprehend who they really are and if they are approaching things in same way that others do in order to find affinity and group identity. Too often, people believe that if they do things differently than others, that they are making a mistake or it is forbidden. Sometimes taking other routes creates pressure and discomfort due to uncertainty related to the new approach that can complicate reaching the goal. SM helps with that because users skip

the physical world and interact with users located in different areas with a different culture and tradition from their own, and that have solved the same situation with different methods. This kind of exchange of information supports society's development because it increases knowledge and experience among the world's population.

3. **Social need.** People want to stay in contact to make their relationships work and benefit from the interaction.

4. The last element identified in this analysis is the desire to reach **practical goals,** in the sense that communication is essential to ask for something (e.g. information, documents, etc) obtain answers, clarify situations, etc. SM are also very valuable in this case because they represent another route for communication in general because they reach a wide audience, they support exchange of documents and information.

SM have **specific characteristics:**

1. They support a global communication;
2. They favour effective and concise messages, this means that few lines are the average for this communication systems in order to keep engaged the receiver.
3. They support instant messaging. This means that the time needed for the message to travel and to reach the receiver is in seconds and this creates the condition for a real time conversation.

Professor Ennis maintains that SM system is vehicle for information that has a high inclination for space-bias. This means that compared to TV, print and radio, it is faster and more effective but, in contrast, it loses in the size of the audience, content length and message detail.

In terms of market growth, market penetration and interest, SM depend, above all, on:

a) Hardware devices;
b) The inclination to use them;
c) The Internet connection.

According to the statistics in this book, there are more mobile device users than desktop ones, and this means that there are more opportunities for people to use SM for their activities. TV remains the first medium for population penetration but spend more time on online content rather than traditional TV.

In general, the newest models of TVs can support SM applications, the purchase of online programs, Skype calls, streaming programs, etc. In this way, traditional media and social media try to coexist and benefit from each other.

As has been said, one of the key characteristics of SM is the ability to spread a message to large communities. Indeed, SM are used by politicians, entrepreneurs and companies to reach their goals. This means that SM have an intrinsic power to communicate directly to the audience, cutting out intermediaries that could increase the *"noise"* during the transmission of the message. From the side of the user, there is the possibility to choose what news you get and from whom. Indeed, before the advent of SM, all news was in the hands of just a few broadcasting companies and news agencies and, in this scenario, the viewers had to wait for a specific time to get the information of interest. Furthermore, the duration of the programs, the prominence of the news and the level of the analysis of these are also decided by broadcasting companies. On the other hand, information based exclusively on SM can mislead the users because they can narrow the information to only few topics.

There are skilled and professional journalists that with their experience are adding value to the news with their comments and analysis. A person who is not a specialist in a specific topic can find it hard to understand a specific situation which can be easily explained by professionals. This means that plurality is the answer; that all media are important for the generation and dissemination of accurate and balanced information, and one of the responsibilities for the users is to check multiple sources the information of interest and do not expect that only one medium is capable to provide a complete and objective information.

People need to understand that these media impact, directly or indirectly, their lives because SM are able to influence: politics, the economy, society, entertainment and information, are influenced by SM.

Specifically, SM are used to influence the mood and opinion of voters. They are used by anyone who holds any form of power (for influencing voters and citizens, keeping or gaining control, defending a personal status) and, by anyone who has no power and demands more rights, justice or equality. In both cases, SM act as a sounding board for people's messages for seeking supporters, and gives more strength to the message itself. I believe that the method to influence mood and opinion is: sending explicit messages, hammering the followers with a large quantity of messages, influencing the crowds with messages based on fear or anger. As happened in the revolts in North Africa and for the elections of presidents, SM have proved to be important in these changes. They also contributed to changing the way to do business, because they made it possible to identify and focus on specific groups of consumers, and refine research for candidates and information about products. Consumers can find information quickly in order to make their decisions. They can also buy goods and services from the place which is more convenient for them, or from who they want and all of this bypassing national borders. On the other hand, companies have fewer boundaries to move from one country to another, basing their decisions on tax benefits, costs and profits. This is made possible because of the ability to spread the tasks all over the world by having one single and common system of business communication that sees the company's employees as one social community.

SM also impact the relationships between people for many reasons; indeed, people realise that their actions, words or ideas can be commented on or exposed publically, eventually hurting their reputation. In some cases they develop phobias that SM are used for spying.

Sometimes the risk is authentic, and this includes companies exposed to hacker attacks.

Apart from that, SM are also used to get to know more people in real life, by finding new connections through mutual friends.

The entertainment industry is using SM to develop a new era of gaming because the combination of them and Virtual Reality contribute to making the games more realistic and keeping groups of players together. In the future, more online games will be available due to a dual benefit for companies, which can contrast pirated games and for players, who have the possibility to play in single or multiplayer mode, have an access to a wide selection of games. SM also provided the opportunity to extend the offerings of games by creating new applications and entertainment for SNs where people pay real money to see their imaginary fields irrigated, buy a service for automatically feeding their virtual animals, or buy virtual goods. For example, the most popular games created for SNs are FarmVille, Mafia Wars, Farm Town and The Sim social.

The information industry has also changed; there is more news coming from non-professionals who post, comment or analyse episodes of daily life and capture images or videos with their mobile devices. The demand of information has also changed because people know where to get the information they want. The products generated by traditional media consider the comments of SM for their transmission and show schedules. But information is not only news; it also involves knowledge development. By this I mean that information is available for purchase, to learn a new activity or to solve a problem. SM have the dual role of being used to generate and store information.

SM have also received much criticism for different aspects. Before going into these findings, it should be remembered that are first of all a group of media, and hence shares traits common to all the other media.

Specifically, SM can cause addiction for users which is manifested in compulsively checking messages, using SM apps and followed by urge of immediate interaction with sender. Because the interaction platforms are supported by appropriate smart devices, this generates a dependency on these as well. The addicted person cannot separate from them and checks them continuously.

The word "addiction" is derived from the Latin meaning "enslaved by", and from a scientific point of view, this happens because of an excessive release of dopamine and the speed that this leads to addiction depends to the speed of request of dopamine, to the quantity of such release and the reliability of it. The addiction influences the brain in three different situations:

1. Strong desire for the object;
2. None or minimum control over the its usage;
3. No fear of possible advert consequences.

As for all other addictions, for example smoking, gambling, shopping, drugs and alcohol, SM addiction can generate chronic disease that impacts the brain.

SM, and the Internet in general, does not create an addiction for a substance but for a behaviour. Contrary to the substance, the behavioural addiction is based on repeated actions to seek pleasure.

This method of pursuing pleasure soon becomes a significant part of daily life, and when the addiction becomes evident they want to perform the activity again.

If not properly used, SM can become the source of other problems, for example: cyber bullying, sexual harassment, disturbing content and fraud. For all of these reasons, is always a good habit to discuss doubts with parents or professional experts as appropriate.

SM have also made the life of users more transparent because it can be shared with others despite their will. This situation encourages a discussion on privacy, which is a very important issue for social networks and the request of personal information for the use of SM applications. The current and the future generations of people, who were born into this context do not know what it means to live a life where personal experiences remain private unless there is a desire to inform others. They, therefore, start from a point even more extreme and that, combined with video surveillance in the street and shops, and electronic payment systems, will make them live in a "Truman Show". There is also the fact to consider that SM are perfect for mass surveillance programs, which can analyse billions of messages and store them based on discretional opinion of unknown responsible. In the wrong hands or for the wrong purposes, they could provide personal information, violate personal and corporate secrets, or manipulate personal will or popular trends.

Another criticism of SM is that they are unnecessary to change society, and this is supported by the fact that historical events, such as revolutions, discoveries and battles for human rights, were possible without SM. I believe that it is too early for this kind of evaluation and, moreover, people have to keep in mind that SM have the unique characteristics of support a fast and concise communication between users. Nowadays, what is well underway is the integration of SM into different devices for work and entertainment. Indeed, the new smart devices are ideal for helping in everyday life and can be used, for example at home and in the car for fitness and transportation. Section 5.2 reported different examples and analyses in this respect, looking deep in the evolutions and future perspectives.

As has been said, SM are a group of powerful tools which can create big opportunities and threats, for these reasons is important to understand how use them and for which scope. Using a quote of Erik Qualman: "What happens in Vegas stays on... Facebook, Twitter, Flickr".

Bibliography

Bibliography

Adler, R. B., & Proctor II, R. F. (2012). *Looking Out Looking In* (Fourteenth ed.). (L. Uhl, Ed.) Canada: Wadsworth, Cengage Learning.

Al Jazeera English. (2011, June 05). *Party advertised on Facebook brings over a thousand* . Retrieved August 03, 2015, from YouTube: https://www.youtube.com/watch?v=xxDTe-T__dQ

Atkinson. (1978). *An Introduction to Motivation.* xxx: Van Nostrad. Auvinen, A.-M. (n.d.). *SOCIAL MEDIA - THE NEW POWER OF POLITICAL INFLUENCE.* Retrieved October 23, 2014, from martenscentre.eu: http://martenscentre.eu/sites/default/files/publication-files/kansio-digital_democracy_-_final_en.pdf

Bauman, Z. (2000). *Liquid Modernity.* Polity Press.

Biennale Venezia, iceberg anti grandi navi, n.d. phothograph, viewed 19 February 2016, http://www.vvox.it/2015/05/05/biennale-venezia-iceberg-anti-grandi-navi/

Brown, V., Clery, E., & Ferguson, C. (2011, May). *Estimating the prevalence.* Retrieved November 23, 2014, from Red balloon

learner:
http://redballoonlearner.co.uk/includes/files/resources/2612
98927_red-balloon-natcen-research-report.pdf

Cameron, J. (Director). (1984). *Terminator 1* [Motion Picture].

Centorrino, M., & Romeo, A. (2012). *Sociologia dei digital media.*
Milan, Italy: FrancoAngeli.

Communication Theory. (2013). *Shannon and Weaver Model of
Communication.* Retrieved August 03, 2014, from
http://communicationtheory.org/shannon-and-weaver-
model-of-communication/

Ditch the Label. (2013). *The annual cyberbullyng survey.* Retrieved
November 26, 2014, from ditchthelabel.org:
http://www.ditchthelabel.org/downloads/the-annual-
cyberbullying-survey-2013.pdf

Dunbar, R., (2010). *How many friends does one person need?.* United
Kindom: Faber and Faber Limited.

ElBaradei, M. (2011, April 21). *The 2011 TIME 100.* Retrieved
November 09, 2014, from time:
http://content.time.com/time/specials/packages/article/0,28
804,2066367_2066369_2066437,00.html

eMarketer. (2014, February). *US Twitter User Base Begins to
Mature.* Retrieved July 24, 2014, from emarketer.com:
http://www.emarketer.com/Article/US-Twitter-User-Base-
Begins-Mature/1010641/2

Emmerson, B. (2014). *Promotion and protection of human rights and
fundamental.* United Nation.

Ericrettberg. (2014). *Six degree of separation.* Retrieved May 28, 2015, from http://www.ericrettberg.com/dataculta/experiential-blog-posts/six-degree-of-separation/

European Court of Human Rights. (1950). European Convention on human rights. *Convention for the Protection of Human Rights and Fundamental Freedoms* (p. 55). Rome: Council of Europe.

Facebook. (2014, March). *Company Info.* Retrieved July 19, 2014, from Facebook.com: http://newsroom.fb.com/company-info/

Facebook. (2014, April 24). *Facebook Reports First Quarter 2014 Results.* Retrieved July 20, 2014, from Facebook.com: http://investor.fb.com/releasedetail.cfm?ReleaseID=842071

Fadek, T. (2011, February 10). *Is Social Media Destroying Public Interaction?* Retrieved October 23, 2014, from Bag News Notes: http://www.bagnewsnotes.com/2011/02/tim-fadek-is-social-media-destroying-public-interaction/

Ferriss, T. (2011). *The 4-Hour Work Week: Escape the 9-5, Live Anywhere and Join the New Rich.* Random House.

Forbes. (2012, October 19). *WhatsApp - The Biggest Social Network You've Never Heard Of.* Retrieved May 22, 2014, from Forbes: http://www.forbes.com/sites/benedictevans/2012/10/19/whatsapp-the-biggest-social-network-youve-never-heard-of/

Freedom House. (2012). *Freedom on the Net.* Retrieved
November 09, 2014, from freedomhouse:
http://www.freedomhouse.org/report/freedom-
net/2012/tunisia

Gladwell, M. (2010, October 4). *Small Change.* Retrieved
December 15, 2014, from The New Yorker:
http://www.newyorker.com/magazine/2010/10/04/small-
change-3?currentPage=all

Goessl, L. (2012, February 4). *Study: Social media more addictive
than cigarettes or alcohol.* Retrieved November 17, 2014, from
DIGITAL JOURNAL:
http://www.digitaljournal.com/article/319011

Greenwald, G. (2013, June 6). *NSA whistleblower Edward
Snowden: 'I don't want to live in a society that does these sort of things'.*
Retrieved December 15, 2014, from YouTube:
https://www.youtube.com/watch?feature=player_embedded
&v=5yB3n9fu-rM#!

Greenwald, G., & MacAskill, E. (2013, June 11). *Boundless
Informant: the NSA's secret tool to track global surveillance data.*
Retrieved January 1, 2014, from theguardian:
http://www.theguardian.com/world/2013/jun/08/nsa-
boundless-informant-global-datamining

Hepburn, N. (2013, January 24). *Life in the age of internet
addiction.* Retrieved November 23, 2014, from The Week:
http://theweek.com/article/index/239243/life-in-the-age-of-
internet-addiction

ilsole24ore. (2013). *Elezioni 2013.* Retrieved November 09,
2014, from ilsole24ore:

http://www.i sole24ore.com/speciali/2013/elezioni/risultati/
politiche/static/italia.shtml

Incitez China (2013, June 14). *The Rise of Mobile Social Media in
China*. Retrieved October 25, 2014, from China Internet
Watch: http://www.chinainternetwatch.com/2264/social-
network-serv ce-huge-market/#more-2264

Index Mundi (2014, July). *China Demographics Profile 2014*.
Retrieved October 26, 2014, from indexmundi:
http://www. ndexmundi.com/china/demographics_profile.ht
ml

Innis, H. A. (1950). *Empire and Communication*. Oxford:
Claredon Press.

Innis, H. A. 2008). *The Bias of Communication* (2nd Revised
edition ed.). Toronto: University of Toronto Press.

Internet Live Stats. (2014, July 1). *List of Countries by Internet
Usage (2014)*. Retrieved October 26, 2014, from
Internetlivestats: http://www.internetlivestats.com/internet-
users/

Laad, G., & Lewis, G. (2012, January). *Role of social media in crisis
communication*. Retrieved July 25, 2014, from
http://gerallewis.com/:
http://gerallewis.com/publications/Role_of_Social_Media_i
n_Crisis_Communication_Jan_2012_Gitanjali_Laad.pdf
Laad, G., & Lewis, G. (2012, January). *Role of Social Media in
Crisis Communication*. Retrieved October 24, 2014, from
geraldlewis:
http://www.geraldlewis.com/publications/Role_of_Social_M
edia_in_Crisis_Communication_Jan_2012_Gitanjali_Laad.pdf

Linked In. (2014). *About LinkedIn*. Retrieved July 19, 2014, from LinkedIn.com: http://press.linkedin.com/about

Lookout. (2012). *Mobile Mindset Study*. Lookout.

MacAskill, E., Borger, J., Hopkins, N., Davies, N., & Ball, J. (2013, June 21). *GCHQ taps fibre-optic cables for secret access to world's communications*. Retrieved December 15, 2014, from theguardian: http://www.theguardian.com/uk/2013/jun/21/gchq-cables-secret-world-communications-nsa

Madden, M., Lenhart, A., Cortesi, S., Gasser, U., Duggan, M., Smith, A., et al. (2013, May 21).

Teens, Social Media, and Privacy. Retrieved December 07, 2014, from pewinternet.org: http://www.pewinternet.org/2013/05/21/teens-social-media-and-privacy/

Meeker, M., & Wu, L. (2013, May 29). *2013 Internet Trends*. Retrieved July 01, 2014, from kpcb.com: http://de.slideshare.net/kleinerperkins/kpcb-internet-trends-2013?ref=http://23moments.com/2013/must-read-mary-meekers-internet-trends-2013/

Meeker, M., (2015, May 27). *2015 Internet Trends 2015 – Code Conference*. Retrieved January 05, 2016, from kpcb.com: http://www.kpcb.com/internet-trends

Millis, J. (2008, December 3). *Couple's £1.5m house trashed after hundreds of Facebook gatecrashers storm daughter's 16th birthday party*. Retrieved December 6, 2014, from Daily Mail :

http://www.dailymail.co.uk/news/article-1091124/Couples-1-5m-house-trashed-hundreds-Facebook-gatecrashers-storm-daughters-16th-birthday-party.html

Ministero dell'Interno. (2013). *ARCHIVIO STORICO DELLE ELEZIONI - Consultazione dati*. Retrieved November 09, 2014, from interno.it: http://elezionistorico.interno.it/index.php

Mitchell, K. J., Jones, L., Finkelhor, D., & Wolak, J. (2014, February). *Trends in Unwanted Online Experiences and Sexting*. Retrieved December 03, 2014, from CACRC: http://www.unh.edu/ccrc/pdf/Full%20Trends%20Report%20Feb%202014%20with%20tables.pdf

National Crime Prevention Council. (n.d.). *Cyberbullying*. Retrieved November 23, 2014, from NCPC: http://www.ncpc.org/topics/cyberbullying

Nielsen. (2012). *The state of media: The social Media Report*. Retrieved November 09, 2014, from nielsen: http://www.nielsen.com/content/dam/corporate/us/en/reports-downloads/2012-Reports/The-Social-Media-Report-2012.pdf

Nielsen. (2014). *The digital consumer*. Retrieved February 18, 2016, from nielsen: http://www.nielsen.com/content/dam/corporate/us/en/reports-downloads/2014%20Reports/the-digital-consumer-report-feb-2014.pdf

Nowotarski, M. (2011, January 23). *Don't Steal My Avatar! Challenges of Social Networking Patents*. Retrieved July 26, 2014, from ipwatchdog.com:

http://www.ipwatchdog.com/2011/01/23/dont-steal-my-avatar-challenges-of-social-networking-patents/id=14531/

Peterson, R. (2012, April 6). *Should Mobile Carriers Limit Access to Social Networks? - See more at: http://www.buzzingup.com/2012/04/should-mobile-carriers-limit-access-social-networks/#sthash.N0rUdnaw.dpuf.* Retrieved November 20, 2013, from buzzingup.com: http://www.buzzingup.com/2012/04/should-mobile-carriers-limit-access-social-networks/

Pew Research Center. (2012, November 15). *Low Marks for the 2012 Election.* Retrieved November 09, 2014, from peoplepress: http://www.people-press.org/files/legacy-pdf/11-15-12%20Post%20Election.pdf

PWC. (2014, August 14). *PwC Global Media Outlook 2014-2018.* Retrieved October 26, 2014, from pwc.com : http://kea-cms.s3.amazonaws.com/events/presentations/000/000/320/original/FINAL_justert_uten_speakernotes_Global_Media_Outlook_20142018_270814.pdf?1409226448

Qualman, E. (2010). *Social Media Revolution 2.* Retrieved June 16, 2014, from Vimeo.com: http://vimeo.com/11551721

RT. (2011). *Assange: Facebook, Google, Yahoo spying tools for US intelligence.* Retrieved December 07, 2014, from You Tube: https://www.youtube.com/watch?v=Hp8rJVWC2a0

Rusche, D. (2013, June 8). *Facebook and Google insist they did not know of Prism surveillance program.* Retrieved December 8, 2014, from theguardian: http://www.theguardian.com/world/2013/jun/07/google-

facebook-prism-surveillance-
program?guri=Article:in%20body%20link

Schalkoff, R. J. (1990). *Artificial Intelligence: An Engineering Approach.* McGraw-Hill.

SHANNON, C. E. (1948, July). A Mathematical Theory of Communication. *Bell System Technical Journal , 27* (3), pp. 379–423.

Shannon, C. E., & Weaver, W. (1969). *The mathematical theory of communication* University of Illinois Press.

Solis, B. (2007, August 28). Retrieved July 18, 2014, from briansolis: http://www.briansolis.com/2007/08/social-media-is-about-sociology-not/

Statista. (2014). *Cable radio and TV penetration rate in China from 2008 to 2012.* Retrieved 2014, from statista: http://www.statista.com/statistics/279104/cable-radio-and-tv-penetration-rate-in-china/

Statista. (2015). *Worldwide mobile app revenues.* Retrieved 2016, from statista: **http://www.statista.com/statistics/269025/worldwide-mobile-app-revenue-forecast/**
Sterne, J. (2010). Social Media Metrics. In J. Sterne, *Social Media Metrics, How to measure and optimize your marketing investment* (pp. XVII-XIX). Hoboken, New Jersey: John Wiley & Sons, Inc.

Team YS. (2013, January 16). *6 Social Media Trends for 2013 ... read more on yourstory.com.* Retrieved 11 8, 2013, from Your

Story: http://yourstory.com/2013/01/6-social-media-trends-for-2013/

The Guardian. (2013, July 31). *XKeyscore presentation from 2008.* Retrieved December 15, 2014, from theguardian.com: http://www.theguardian.com/world/interactive/2013/jul/31/nsa-xkeyscore-program-full-presentation

Twitter. (2016). *About Twitter.* Retrieved 2016, from twitter: https://about.twitter.com/en/company

UN News Centre. (2014, October 23). *Right to online privacy at risk as governments engage in mass surveillance – UN expert.* Retrieved December 07, 2014, from un.org: http://www.un.org/apps/news/story.asp?NewsID=49156#.VIR8YzHz1yF

World Bank Group. (2013). *China Data.* Retrieved October 26, 2014, from worldbank: http://data.worldbank.org/country/china

www.ingramcontent.com/pod-product-compliance
Lightning Source LLC
LaVergne TN
LVHW092334060326
832902LV00008B/642